I0455478

CONTENTS

i

FOREWORD

Western military forces and security and intelligence agencies are justifiably concerned about two phenomena that continue to affect their ongoing asymmetric conflicts with jihadist terrorist organizations: 1) the increasing diffusion and application of expertise acquired by jihadists in fabricating "improvised explosive devices" (IEDs), and 2) the extent to which local jihadist cells in the West may or may not be connected to veteran terrorist groups and networks in other countries and regions. This monograph by Dr. Jeffrey M. Bale argues that these two issues are, in fact, interrelated. Using the March 2004 Madrid train bombings and the two failed July 2006 train bombings near Cologne as contrasting case studies, Bale argues that jihadist cells whose members are linked organizationally, logistically, or operationally to wider terrorist networks, especially ones comprising well-trained and battle-tested operatives, are much more likely to be able to acquire the levels of technical expertise needed to manufacture effective IEDs, carry out devastatingly successful single IED attacks, and perhaps even sustain longer-term IED bombing campaigns.

Although these conclusions might seem to be self-evident, they, in fact, challenge the widespread notions that amateur would-be bomb makers using the Internet are likely to be able to carry out highly destructive IED attacks or IED campaigns without having received any hands-on training from professionals, and that today supposedly "self-generating" jihadist cells made up of "bunches of [regular] guys" with no significant connections to larger networks of extremists constitute the principal terrorist threat to the West. Although autonomous groups of relative amateurs,

iii

or even ideologically-motivated lone individuals, can occasionally carry out one or two devastating bomb attacks, cause significant casualties, and create other security problems because they may be able to operate "under the radar" beforehand, the most serious terrorist threats, IED or otherwise, stem from jihadist cells with a web of interconnections to networks of veteran terrorists, including those with operational and bomb making expertise. As a result, determining the type and degree of connectivity between particular jihadist cells and wider terrorist networks is of great importance in assessing their probable operational effectiveness. In order to shed more light on this matter, Bale develops a new categorization scheme herein for assessing different types and levels of local cell connectivity.

This monograph was funded by the Department of Defense in connection with a larger project the purpose of which was to help military units and security agencies better assess and cope with the growing IED threat, both overseas and at home.

DOUGLAS C. LOVELACE, JR.
Director
Strategic Studies Institute

ABOUT THE AUTHOR

JEFFREY M. BALE is the Director of the Monterey Terrorism Research and Education Program (MonTREP) and an Associate Professor in the Graduate School of International Policy and Management (GSIPM) at the Monterey Institute of International Studies (MIIS). Dr. Bale has been studying violence-prone political and religious extremists for nearly 3 decades—long before it suddenly became "fashionable" in the wake of the tragic September 11, 2001 (9/11) attacks on the United States. He has published numerous scholarly articles on nonstate and state terrorism, right-wing extremism, Islamism, apocalyptic religious groups, and covert political operations, and (together with Bassam Tibi) co-edited a special June 2009 issue of the journal *Totalitarian Movements and Political Religions* (recently renamed *Politics, Religion & Ideology*) devoted to Islamism. He is in the process of updating a two-part manuscript on underground neo-fascist networks in Cold War Europe and the terrorist "strategy of tension" in Italy, and preparing three new scholarly monographs: one (for Routledge) on the growing links between dissident left- and right-wing radicals in the West and Islamist groups (*Where the Extremes Touch*); another (also for Routledge) on the burgeoning "conspiracy theory" literature related to 9/11 and other major recent terrorist attacks (*Imagined Terrorist Plots*); and still another on the ideological background and organizational connections of Norwegian terrorist Anders Behring Breivik (*A Strange Tale of Rival Right-Wing Extremisms*). Dr. Bale has carried out specialized archival research in the United States as well as in several European countries, has personally interviewed extremists from several political and religious milieus, and has accumulated an extensive collection of primary source materials related to both extremist and terrorist groups and covert politics. He frequently serves as a consultant and researcher for government agencies and other organizations on matters related to terrorism and ideological extremism, and regularly teaches on a visiting basis at the Naval Postgraduate School (NPS). He previously taught at the University of California, Berkeley; Columbia University; and the University of California, Irvine. Dr. Bale holds a B.A. in Middle Eastern and Islamic history from the University of Michigan, an M.A. in social movements and political sociology from the University of California, Berkeley, and a Ph.D. in contemporary European history from Berkeley.

SUMMARY

During the past 2 decades, two interrelated security threats have emerged that Western democracies will likely be forced to contend with for the foreseeable future. The first of these threats is multifaceted inasmuch as it stems from a complex combination of religious, political, historical, cultural, social, and economic motivational factors: the growing predilection for carrying out mass casualty terrorist attacks inside the territories of "infidel" Western countries by clandestine operational cells that are inspired ideologically by, and sometimes linked organizationally to, various jihadist networks with a global agenda. The most important of these latter networks is still the late Usama bin Ladin's high-profile group Qa'idat al-Jihad (The Base [or Foundation] of the Jihad), together with its many organizational offshoots and regional affiliates. The second threat is more narrowly technical: the widespread fabrication of increasingly sophisticated and destructive improvised explosive devices (IEDs) by those very same jihadist groups, devices which—if properly constructed—are capable of causing extensive human casualties and significant amounts of physical destruction within their respective blast radiuses. The purpose of this monograph is to examine these dual intersecting threats within the recent European context in an effort to assess what they might portend for the future, including the U.S. homeland.

JIHADIST CELLS AND "IED" CAPABILITIES IN EUROPE: ASSESSING THE PRESENT AND FUTURE THREAT TO THE WEST

BACKGROUND

During the past 2 decades, two interrelated security threats have emerged that Western democracies will likely be forced to contend with for the foreseeable future. The first of these threats is multifaceted inasmuch as it stems from a complex combination of religious, political, historical, cultural, social, and economic motivational factors: the growing predilection for carrying out mass casualty terrorist attacks inside the territories of "infidel" Western countries by clandestine operational cells that are inspired ideologically by, and sometimes linked organizationally to, various jihadist networks with a global agenda. The most important of these latter networks is Usama bin Ladin's high-profile group Qa'idat al-Jihad (The Base [or Foundation] of the Jihad), together with its many organizational offshoots and affiliates. The second threat is more narrowly technical: the widespread fabrication of increasingly sophisticated and destructive improvised explosive devices (IEDs) by those very same jihadist groups, devices which (if properly constructed) are capable of causing extensive human casualties and significant amounts of physical destruction within their respective blast radiuses. The purpose of this monograph is to examine these dual intersecting threats, above all within the recent European context, in an effort to assess what they might portend for the future, including for the U.S. homeland. Specifically, the goal herein will be to assess the extent to which members of more or less autonomous jihadist cells are likely to be able to make a transition from carrying out single attacks with IEDs, which some analysts believe is not particularly difficult, to launching more sustained "IED campaigns," which most specialists agree would require considerably more expertise and resources to manage.

PART I:

INTRODUCTION

This monograph is organized into four parts. Part I seeks to clarify various preliminary conceptual issues, ranging from the appropriateness of the definitions of improvised explosive devices (IEDs) to the factors involved in their employment and diffusion. Part II deals, relatively briefly, with the question of whether would-be jihadists can fabricate an effective, sophisticated, or destructive IED merely by following the instructions in a hard copy or online instruction manual, or whether they generally need to get hands-on technical training from an experienced bombmaker in order to be able to make really devastating devices. Part III, the heart of the report, deals with the thorny question of whether jihadist cells in Europe really are amateur "self-starter" groups of kinsmen and friends that are not linked organically to professional terrorist networks, as Marc Sageman argues; whether they generally are linked to such networks, as Bruce Hoffman suggests; or whether they fit into neither of those paradigms comfortably. This is necessary because determining the level of professionalism of cell members is likely to be of seminal importance if one is attempting to assess their capabilities for: (1) manufacturing sophisticated IEDs, and (2) launching sustained IED campaigns. Hence two illustrative cases are examined herein in more detail. Part IV then offers some tentative conclusions that might enable security officials to formulate more accurate threat assessments concerning potential future IED attacks and campaigns in the West.

DEFINITIONAL AND CONCEPTUAL PROBLEMS WITH THE TERM "IMPROVISED EXPLOSIVE DEVICE"

The first key issue to be dealt with is how, precisely, to define and delimit the application of the term "Improvised Explosive Device." According to the definition being used by the National Academies, the term seems to refer both to: (1) explosive devices that are hand-made, artisanal, or "improvised" with respect to their manufacture, i.e., that are not prefabricated according to specifications on a factory assembly line, like conventional military munitions, or (2) conventional explosive devices, including military grade explosives and military munitions (e.g., artillery shells) that are used in innovative, unconventional, or improvised ways, i.e., not in the way in which they are designed for use in the course of conventional military operations but rather in an unconventional manner in the context of irregular, unconventional, or asymmetric warfare.[1] While one need not object in principle to this sort of formulation, the problem is that virtually any kind of explosive device that is manufactured or used by nonstate groups in more or less nonconventional ways can now be placed willy-nilly into the "IED" category. This raises two questions: (1) are there any types of explosive devices used by insurgent or irregular forces that do *not* fall into the "improvised" category, and, (2) if not, have we simply created a trendy new buzzword covering every type of bombing carried out by guerrillas, insurgents, irregulars, and terrorists?

Given the penchant for creating acronyms by U.S. Government agencies, especially the Department of Defense (DoD), does the use of the term IED really add any precision or "scientific" value to earlier ways of describing or characterizing such devices or attacks? For example, is there any advantage in employing the term Vehicle-Borne Improvised Explosive Device (VBIED) to refer to an old-fashioned car or truck bomb, or in using the term Person-Borne Improvised Explosive Device (PBIED) to refer to a "suicide bomber"? One wonders.

The second conceptual point to make is that IEDs, however the term is defined, can be employed both in "normal" instrumental acts of violence (e.g., simply to eliminate, destroy, or damage particular human and nonhuman targets) and in bona fide acts of terrorism, i.e., acts of violence *for psychological effect* in which the perpetrators' primary purpose is to influence the perceptions and behavior of a wider target audience or audiences.[2] It is important to distinguish conceptually between standard acts of violence that involve only two parties, the perpetrator(s) and the victim(s), which technically do not constitute acts of terrorism, and acts of terrorist violence which invariably involve three parties, the perpetrator(s), the victim(s), and the wider target audience(s) upon whom the perpetrator(s) intentionally aim to exert a psychological impact. Given their dramatic effects and destructive power, IEDs are obviously well suited for both types of attacks.[3]

UNDER WHAT CIRCUMSTANCES DO NONSTATE GROUPS EMPLOY IEDS?

When considering the prior and likely future use of IEDs in attacks by insurgents or terrorists, one must carefully evaluate the role played by: (1) operational objectives; (2) ideological factors; (3) organizational factors, which are especially relevant to the matter of operational capabilities and available resources; and (4) environmental and contextual factors.

Operational Objectives and IED Use.

There is no real mystery about why particular insurgent groups (or, for that matter, their opponents) have often had recourse to making and employing IEDs. The primary reasons why diverse extremist and opposition groups have chosen to employ such devices are that IEDs are relatively easy to manufacture and deploy, relatively cheap to fabricate, and have repeatedly proven, in a multitude of different historical, cultural, and operational contexts, to be highly effective.[4] Explosive devices, improvised or not, enable the groups employing them—assuming that their members are minimally competent in operational and technical matters—to successfully attack and harm their targets or, in the case of terrorism proper, to affect the psychological state, perceptions, and behavior of the target audiences they are trying to influence. In short, from a narrowly tactical or operational point of view, the decision to employ IEDs often appears to be quite rational: Groups believe that they can get a lot of "bang for the buck" and thereby accomplish their operational objectives. *Hence the difficult question to answer is not so much why certain groups might use IEDs, but rather why other groups might decide* not *to.* From a strictly operational standpoint, the only reasons why groups might refrain from using IEDs is because they fear alienating the sympathies of their base of supporters by carrying out indiscriminate bomb attacks, or they have already become accustomed to using and hence continue to prefer to use other signature tactics that they consider effective. In other words, the "operational signature" or "operational profile" of particular groups is in certain cases based on the use of other types of weapons and tactics, not IEDs. For example, the leftist Brigate Rosse (Red Brigades [BR]) preferred to kidnap, "kneecap," or assassinate individuals whom they felt were representatives of the "imperialist state of the multinationals," i.e., functionaries of the "oppressive" capitalist class or the "bourgeois" democratic state which was supposedly beholden to that class. The BR did not have any fundamental ideological objections to or moral qualms about using explosives, but it was simply not the group's preferred tactic.[5] Moreover, recent self-proclaimed offshoots of the BR, the so-called "new" BR, have likewise not yet resorted to mass casualty attacks or the use of sophisticated IEDs, even though one of those offshoots — the Nuclei Territoriali Antiimperialisti (Anti-Imperialist Territorial Cells [NTA]) — has bombed several parked automobiles and specifically advocated an alliance between Western left-wing radicals and the "anti-imperialist" fighter Usama bin Ladin.[6] This suggests that the mere diffusion of IED knowledge and technology will not necessarily cause extremist groups that have historically preferred other methods to employ IEDs in mass casualty attacks.

Ideological Factors in IED Use.

The question here is whether particular extremist or insurgent groups have any moral reservations about, or ideological/theological objections to, the likely causing of inadvertent loss of life (collateral damage) or mass casualties as a result of IED attacks. In the case of jihadist groups, however, this is not an issue: They have neither moral nor ideological objections to carrying out public bombings using IEDs against "infidels," including within the *dar al-harb* (abode of war, i.e., portions of the world in which the *shari'a* does not hold sway and where unbelievers are not paying the *jizya* or poll tax to signal their submission), because they believe that both killing and terrorizing infidels is specifically sanctioned by passages in the *Qur'an* and/or by supporting *ahadith* (accounts of what Muhammad allegedly said or did).[7] Furthermore, on the basis of Islamic "just war" conceptions of proportionality with respect both to scope and means, jihadist spokesmen have openly proclaimed that they have the right to kill millions of Americans, including by means of the use of so-called "weapons of mass destruction" (WMD).[8] Moreover, both Usama bin Ladin and Ayman al-Zawahiri have sought to provide explicit theological-legal justifications for killing both American civilians (including women and children) and Muslims who are living in targeted regions of the *dar al-harb*.[9] Add to that a host of semi-rational or non-rational "expressive" impulses or motives, e.g., a desire to cleanse the world of corruption by exterminating unbelievers, obsessions with getting revenge for real or imagined crimes, a passion for martyrdom, or the desire to precipitate an apocalyptic end-of-days scenario, and one can easily conclude that the jihadists have no ideological restraints whatsoever that might inhibit them from causing mass, indiscriminate casualties.[10] If such repeated pronouncements are not alone sufficient to convince every careful observer, all one has to do is look at their normal *modus operandi*, which is characterized by the widespread employment of IEDs to cause mass casualties and/or traumatize target audiences on virtually every front where jihadists are waging armed struggle, from Algeria to Iraq, from Afghanistan to Chechnya, from Kashmir to Thailand, and from Europe to Indonesia.

Organizational Factors in IED Use.

In many contexts the most important organizational issue that could affect the use and impact of future IED attacks is the extent to which the jihadist groups emerging in particular areas have had or will in the future develop tangible links to more professional terrorist networks and groups, either in their own region or elsewhere. Most analysts have been fixated on the question of whether Qa'idat al-Jihad has provided, or will henceforth be providing, direct or indirect operational and logistical assistance to home-grown jihadist cells in other parts of the world, but it would be a serious mistake to overlook or minimize the possible connections between newly-formed jihadist cells and professional terrorist groups based in places like Morocco, Algeria, Egypt, Chechnya, or Kashmir. At this juncture, debates continue to rage between those researchers who argue that many, if not most, of the supposed "self-starter" jihadist groups in various regions have in fact had documented links to cadres of Qa'idat al-Jihad, which in its most extreme formulations could lead to the conclusion that Usama bin Ladin and his organization's *majlis al-shura* (consultative council) are directly ordering, tangibly assisting, or even secretly "teleguiding" jihadist attacks in various countries, and those who claim that the attacking cells, although clearly inspired by the ideology of global jihad (specifically jihadist Salafism), were not connected organizationally or logistically to Qa'idat al-Jihad.[11] As will later become clear, the actual situation on the ground generally lies somewhere between these two interpretive poles—e.g., at least two members of the "bunch of guys" that carried out the 7/7 suicide bombings in London reportedly traveled to Pakistan and made contact with jihadist militants there, including those at a Lashkar-i Tayyiba (Army of the Pure [LeT]) *madrasa* near Lahore[12]—but this sort of question obviously cannot be answered in a general or abstract way: *Only careful and thorough qualitative empirical research on a case-by-case basis can shed sufficient light on these complex matters*, and each case is likely to be different from the others and, virtually by definition, unique in certain respects. One single interpretative framework therefore does not and cannot fit every individual case, though after carefully examining a variety of such cases one may eventually be able to discern and identify broader trends.

The reason why this organizational issue may well be of considerable importance is because it seems a priori probable that cells connected in various ways with veteran, professional terrorist groups or networks, or whose members have received hands-on instruction in jihadist training camps, would be better able to construct more effective IEDs (in terms of their overall destructive power and anti-personnel effects) and/or plan more devastatingly effective attacks, e.g., a near simultaneous series of bombings, bombings involving secondary and tertiary explosions that are designed to kill emergency personnel and onlookers who rush to the scene of the initial bombing, a more skillful deployment of chemical agents or radiological dispersion devices (RDDs), etc. This does not mean, of course, that a small group of resourceful (and perhaps lucky) amateurs would necessarily be unable to carry out a highly destructive and bloody attack that ended up having a traumatic psychological impact or affecting government policies. If one accepts the problematic thesis of Marc Sageman and Scott Atran, for example, that the Madrid bombings were carried out by a relatively amateurish "bunch of guys" with only tenuous links to other jihadist organizations — a topic that will be investigated further below[13] — it is obvious that even amateurs can carry out a highly successful, near simultaneous bomb attack using fairly simple homemade IEDs. However, even if a particular "self-starter" group was able to carry out one successful IED attack, even a major one, it is questionable whether it would be able to carry out sustained IED campaigns.

Environmental and Contextual Factors in IED Use.

The continent of Europe, like North America, constitutes an almost ideal operating environment within which to plan and carry out IED attacks. Apart from the fact that jihadists consider all of Europe (excepting Bosnia and Albania) to be "infidel territory" and most European governments to be key participants in the "Zionist-Crusader war against Islam," European countries offer many other advantages as IED targets. First, they are unusually rich in targets of both tangible and symbolic importance, ranging from sophisticated public transportation systems that ferry millions of civilians back and forth on a daily basis, to the innumerable symbols of Europe's past glory (such as the Vatican) and present power (such as financial centers and military bases). Second, the freedoms provided by Western democratic societies enable extremist and subversive groups of various types, including Islamist networks, to operate with relative freedom of action and impunity (despite the prodigious and sometimes effective efforts of various European secret services to monitor their activities). In particular, Islamist radicals (including future would-be jihadists) find it easy to exploit the European legal and welfare systems to promote their extremist agendas and engage in anti-democratic activities, and they likewise find it relatively easy to "hide in plain sight" in ghettoized Muslim communities on the peripheries of major European cities.[14] Moreover, even when they are arrested and brought to trial, the nature of European judicial systems and the political proclivities of many judges often combine to make it hard to prosecute them successfully. So it is that such radicals can systematically take advantage of the very freedoms that they detest in order to identify, conduct surveillance of, and eventually attack a multitude of potentially vulnerable and highly-desirable targets.

PRELIMINARY THOUGHTS ON IED DIFFUSION: HOW ARE IED KNOW-HOW AND TECHNOLOGY SPREAD?

At first glance one might either assume or hypothesize that information about how to construct IEDs, or the actual technologies needed to fabricate them, would be likely to spread in one of two ways. First, they could spread outward from particular geographic locales where insurgents or terrorists had already developed a certain amount of expertise in constructing and employing IEDs (or perhaps where they had access to certain materials needed to manufacture them that were unavailable elsewhere), which would mean that one could probably trace their diffusion spatially from particular geographic centers, first to adjacent and thence to further removed territories. This would also imply that, temporally, those techniques would spread outward through a relatively gradual process. Second, they could be spread in conjunction with the movements of particular individuals who already had expertise in creating and deploying IEDs, whether those movements conformed to predictable patterns or were more random. In such a situation, the spread of IED know-how would not necessarily be characterized by a gradually expanding process of diffusion outwards from a particular epicenter, but instead move along the circuitous paths taken by those individuals. In that sense, knowledge would be more likely to "jump" spatially and thereby be transmitted somewhat more rapidly than in the aforementioned diffusion pattern. For example, if an IED expert traveled from al-'Anbar province in Iraq to a destination in Europe or Southeast Asia, his knowledge and expertise would be likely to move and potentially be spread along with him. But this would not necessarily follow an easily discernible pattern, and unless U.S. intelligence agencies were somehow able to monitor the movements of such individuals it might be very difficult for them to glean where and when this accumulated know-how might appear or be transmitted next. In this second type of "personal" diffusion, the appropriate analogy might be to tracing the spread of infectious diseases by following the travel itineraries of infected individuals.

However, in today's Internet era, the processes of IED knowledge and technology diffusion are arguably less likely to conform to such traditional patterns of technological diffusion. Unfortunately, it is now possible for individuals all over the world to access the Internet and get information therein about how to obtain chemicals and other materials needed for IEDs, as well as detailed instructions for actually fabricating them. In short, the diffusion of rudimentary IED know-how no longer primarily depends, as it generally had in earlier eras, on its gradual expansion outwards from specific geographic nodes, the physical movements of knowledgeable and experienced people, or, perhaps, on the potentially traceable and therefore risky acquisition of obscure and often illegal hard copy bomb making manuals. Nowadays locating information about how to construct home-made bombs is as easy as clicking on a URL from a desktop or portable computer, perhaps one at an Internet café on which time has been rented under a fictive name and paid for with cash. This is certainly something that many "wanna-be" jihadists do these days.

Perhaps the most important question, then, is whether one needs to obtain actual hands-on training from an explosives expert to be able to construct highly effective IEDs, or whether one can do so simply by carefully following the instructions provided in an online IED manual. This is a question that technical experts are perhaps best able to answer, although one would suspect that efforts by rank amateurs to learn how to construct and deploy IEDs, especially amateurs without any prior scientific or technical background, are in general not likely to lead to optimal results in terms of achieving their operational objectives, whether those objectives be causing mass casualties, destroying targeted facilities, traumatizing target audiences, or some combination thereof. Indeed, efforts by untrained amateurs to fabricate IEDs solely from online instructional materials are likely to lead, perhaps not infrequently, either to premature accidental detonations and the resultant maiming or death of the would-be bomb-maker, or to the mistaken fabrication of bombs that then fail to detonate. Moreover, until they have acquired more firsthand operational experience in deploying IEDs and created an efficient logistical infrastructure of some type, it will likely be more difficult for self-styled revolutionaries or *"mujahidin"* to launch sustained IED campaigns even if they are capable of launching successful single IED attacks.

Of course, one of the main characteristics of IEDs is that they are "improvised." This implies that there are innumerable new and creative ways to make explosive devices by employing a wide variety of chemicals and household objects, not to mention actual military munitions. In that sense, it may not always be the slavish imitation of devices and techniques that have previously been used and disseminated by others, including professional bombmakers, but rather the innovative development of entirely new types of devices and techniques by clever amateurs with technical skills, which ends up creating significant new terrorist threats. In that sense, the only certain limits that can be placed on the ability to construct and deploy IEDs, apart from the laws of physics and access to a minimal amount of resources, are those of the human imagination itself. As has already become clear in Iraq, different groups of insurgents are both very adaptive and very innovative in terms of employing locally available materials in creative ways and devising techniques to circumvent U.S. efforts to discover IEDs, dismantle them, or jam the signals that are used to detonate them. At a 2006 conference in Monterey, California, a British munitions expert explained just how easy it was to fabricate devastatingly effective IEDs, how difficult it was to identify, disarm, or defuse them, and how adaptable the insurgents had become in finding ways to deal with sophisticated Coalition countermeasures, both human and technical. This provides yet another illustration, if any was needed, that the ongoing process of mutual learning and adaptation between adversaries in warfare shows no signs of abating.[15] It also indicates that battle-hardened and creative insurgents, however rigid and fanatical they may be from an ideological standpoint, can eventually find ways of adapting or effectively responding, in the operational realm, to the immense technological superiority of U.S. and Western armies, and that a complex array of human factors, both tangible and intangible, will remain decisive elements in the outcome of present and future conflicts.

PART II:

INDIVIDUAL AND ORGANIZATIONAL LEARNING ABOUT IEDs

Not all terrorists learn, and those that do appear limited in their ability to do so.

— Michael Kenney[16]

One issue raised in the introduction was whether members of terrorist cells would need to receive direct personal training from individuals with actual expertise, i.e., with significant prior hands-on bombmaking experience, in order to learn how to fabricate effective improvised explosive devices (IEDs) themselves. It would be rash to draw categorical conclusions about this matter, since certain talented amateurs have in the past sometimes been capable — and will no doubt in the future also sometimes be capable — of manufacturing very destructive IEDs, either by imaginatively applying their existing levels of technical knowledge or by following detailed step-by-step instructions found in manuals, even without having had the benefit of direct personal instruction from an experienced bombmaker. Nevertheless, the question is not whether such amateurs might occasionally be able to fabricate such devices, which is a certainty, but rather how frequently they are likely to be able to do so.

Hence a brief discussion should be undertaken about the general importance of individual learning and organizational learning in terrorist groups. Alas, not enough in-depth research has as yet been carried out on the specific processes by which members of terrorist groups, or their organizations as a whole, actually acquire, analyze, share, and apply knowledge, in part because most of the existing literature on social learning and organizational behavior has been focused on relatively large, stable, formal, and bureaucratized organizations instead of on small, sectarian, violence-prone political or religious groups that are compelled to operate clandestinely or covertly in hostile law enforcement and military environments. Such groups are usually characterized by ideological extremism, authoritarian and often charismatic leadership, insularity, internal factionalism leading to organizational fission and fusion, compartmentalization on a need-to-know basis, and intense intra-group social dynamics. Oftentimes, it has simply been assumed that terrorist groups will continue to learn, like most supposedly "rational" actors, as time progresses. However, there is no doubt that different terrorist groups, including those that emerge from within the same ideological milieu, do not all learn vital skills and important lessons at the same rate. Nor, for that matter, do they all learn equally well. Thus it should not simply be assumed a priori that particular terrorist groups are invariably learning what they need to know and then effectively applying what they have learned, all the more so given that social learning tends to be "sensitive to a variety of individual and institutional impediments, including bounded rationality, coalition dynamics, and organizational inertia."[17]

However that may be, in the context of both individual learning and organizational learning, an important preliminary distinction must be drawn between what has generally been referred to as "explicit knowledge" and that which has been dubbed "tacit knowledge."[18] Explicit knowledge refers to formal knowledge about how to do something that can be effectively codified in various formats and can thence be transmitted easily to others. In contrast, tacit knowledge is more informal personalized knowledge gained through sometimes unique individual experiences, which often manifests itself in the form of subjective insights, intuitions, and hunches, that are harder to formalize and hence much harder to transmit fully to others.[19] An example of explicit knowledge, with respect to IEDs, would be the information found in hard copy or online manuals that provide detailed instructions about how to make bombs. An example of tacit knowledge would be the "tricks of the trade" painstakingly acquired over a period of years by veteran, highly-skilled bomb makers, which are likely to include all sorts of innovative, flexible, and adaptive techniques, nuances, and insights, many of them idiosyncratic, that are not to be found in standardized manuals. Diligent students might eventually succeed in learning the basics of bomb making from such manuals, but they would only be able to learn and master the many subtleties associated with tacit knowledge if they received personal training from, or perhaps even became the protégés of, an experienced bomb maker or, alternatively, after practicing extensively for a considerable period of time and thereby acquiring valuable firsthand experience. Moreover, according to a team of RAND Corporation experts, "[a]cquiring new information, knowledge, or technology from an explicit source is usually only a group's first step. The group must then develop enough tacit knowledge within its ranks to be able to apply the information effectively."[20]

Another, older scheme that was designed to draw a distinction between book learning and experiential learning has recently been resuscitated by Michael

Kenney, who argues that the terms explicit and tacit knowledge should be replaced by the ancient Greek terms *techne* and *mētis*. Although *techne* is very similar to the notion of explicit knowledge, in that it focuses on abstract technical knowledge or "know what" that is structured in "small, explicit, logical steps" which can be broken down, verified, and therefore easily communicated, *mētis* is arguably a more subtle, nuanced version of tacit knowledge.[21] Like the latter, *mētis* focuses on intuitive, practical knowledge or experiential "know how" that one acquires by doing, but it especially emphasizes that this involves a "cunning" or "crafty" intelligence which is manifested through traits such as dexterity, ingenuity, improvisation, and overall adaptability.[22] Such attributes must be present to enable insurgent terrorists to learn quickly and respond effectively to government countermeasures. Unlike *techne*, which consists of codified knowledge that can be acquired by "reading manuals and other documents that provide detailed, step-by-step" instructions, *mētis* must be shared—to the extent that it can be shared—by experienced practitioners through sustained interaction with others, including less experienced acolytes.[23] In the words of Kenney:

> 'Veterans' tell 'novices' stories about their past experiences; they demonstrate how to perform specific tasks; and they mentor aspiring fanatics by building social relationships with them. Like tailors, midwives, butchers, and photocopy technicians, terrorists share *mētis* by participating in 'communities of practice,' social communities formed by veterans and novices that interact on a regular basis, creating and re-creating experiential knowledge expressed in shared narratives, practices, and routines.[24]

This distinction between *techne* and *mētis* is obviously very relevant to the terrorist use of IEDs.

Thus far the focus has been on the individual learning of bomb making and related skills, but it is necessary to emphasize that organizational learning is also of vital importance for terrorist organizations. This is because insurgent terrorist groups operate within a fluid, dynamic, and adversarial conflict environment characterized by interactive processes of thrust-and-parry, action-and-reaction, or response-and-counter-response — in short, a complex process of "competitive adaptation" — between their own operatives and the security forces of the regimes they are fighting.[25] If they do not continue to learn and adapt, insurgent groups are not likely to be able to prevail against the generally superior forces and greater resources fielded by the state. What is being referred to herein as organizational learning has been defined by Brian Jackson and a team of RAND researchers as "a process through which a group acquires new knowledge or technology that it then uses to make better strategic decisions, improve its ability to develop and apply specific tactics, and increase its chance of success in its operations."[26] These same authors further emphasize that "learning at the organizational level is more than simply the sum of what each individual member knows or can do [because an] organization is *a system that structures, stores, and influences what and how its members learn.*"[27]

It follows that in order to learn, terrorist groups, as organizations, must engage in some process to ensure that the information they acquire is effectively processed and applied. The RAND researchers have characterized this as a fourfold process that involves *acquiring* information and knowledge from both external and internal sources; *interpreting* that information properly; *distributing* it to members of the organization that need access to that information; and then *storing* the information through various means for future collective retrieval.[28] The information that has thereby been learned and retained can then be used to facilitate the group's ability to perform several vitally important functions — to develop, improve, or employ new weapons or tactics in order to change its capabilities over time; to improve the skills of its members so that they can better apply current weapons or tactics; to collect and utilize the intelligence information needed to mount operations effectively; to thwart countermeasures and hence improve its chance to survive efforts to destroy it; and to preserve the capabilities it has already developed even if key individual members are lost.[29] If it is able to build significant expertise within the group, whether through learning by doing, offering basic or specialized training to raise the skill sets of its members and thereby reduce their chances of making mistakes, or carrying out after action reviews to learn from its past successes and failures, it will be able to increase its operational effectiveness considerably and thereafter carry out increasingly destructive and/or complex attacks.[30]

Note, however, that the organizational learning processes discussed by Jackson and his colleagues might be more relevant and applicable to larger insurgent terrorist groups with greater resources than to small, more or less autonomous jihadist cells.[31] Smaller, more transitory ad hoc groups may not need to survive for as long a period, much less to evolve and become increasingly effective, especially if their handful of members intend to martyr themselves in the process of carrying out a terrorist attack. If, on the other hand, they hope to survive, sustain themselves, and remain active for a longer period, they too would benefit from instituting a process of organizational learning, albeit on a smaller scale, in order to increase their operational capabilities and successfully adapt and respond to changing situations. Even in that case, however, the fact that these types of cellular organizations are relatively tiny means that the mechanisms necessary to maintain organizational learning, and in particular to distribute knowledge to members and store it collectively, are likely to be far more rudimentary. In such a case all that is arguably necessary is for key personnel, including bomb makers and operational leaders, to survive so that the cell can maintain itself in being, recruit new members, and continue to operate.

Hence, in the context of small ad hoc jihadist cells in Europe, organizational learning—in contrast to individual learning—might at first sight appear to be less difficult to attain than would be the case for larger, more dispersed, and more functionally specialized terrorist organizations. On the other hand, precisely because such cells are small, geographically concentrated, and relatively noncompartmentalized, they may be far more vulnerable to penetration, covert manipulation, or eventual destruction by the security forces. For that very reason, the maintenance of tight organizational and operational security is perhaps even more essential, at least in the short term, precisely because of the relative paucity of skilled personnel in such cells. After all, if the only effective organizer, operational planner, or experienced bomb maker within a cell is captured or killed, that alone might make it impossible for the remaining members to carry out successful terrorist attacks.

In contrast to the scheme presented by Jackson and his team, Kenney has instead formulated a three-stage process of terrorist organizational learning. From this perspective, "individuals acting on behalf of collectives gather, share, and apply information and experience to their activities, frequently in response to environmental feedback."[32] He also emphasizes that the actual mechanisms associated with this process are related to certain characteristics of jihadist terrorist groups:

> Existing research suggests that jihadists and terrorists connect to like-minded militants through friendship and kinship ties, as well as social affiliations based on common religious or ethnonational backgrounds, geographic proximity, and shared experiences. Network ties among participating "nodes" are sustained and deepened through regular interactions, including communication, information sharing, and coordination of collective action.[33]

Yet how, precisely, do these social network connections and interactions facilitate individual and organizational learning? In general, Kenney argues that terrorists learn by *acquiring* information about various methods (including by gaining firsthand experience employing them), *sharing* knowledge about different operational and technical methods with other trusted persons through varying types of social interaction, and then *applying* that knowledge and experience when planning and carrying out future operations.[34] More specifically, they do so by means of ongoing interactions within the social networks they belong to, by forming "communities of practice," and—to a lesser extent—by consulting the Internet to obtain information. As noted above, communities of practice are formed when experienced veterans begin, more or less systematically, interacting with and providing instruction to novices. After receiving a certain amount of training, the latter then increasingly refine their "knowledge in practice" as they continue to apply the lessons they have learned (assuming that they live to fight another day). In so doing, those who were once novices eventually develop sufficient expertise themselves to become "full-fledged practitioners" in that community of practice.[35] Again, it is within these terrorist communities of practice that the difficult-to-codify and -master skills associated with *mētis* are normally passed on, either directly or indirectly, to less experienced members of particular organizations and cells.

This does not necessarily mean, of course, that jihadist terrorists are always or even normally good at learning, either on the individual or the organizational level. Indeed, one of Kenney's most interesting research findings was that members of the jihadist cells whose activities he examined had often failed to master basic tradecraft skills, both in regard to technical and operational matters, and that consequently they frequently made serious errors when planning and carrying out their attacks.[36] There were many reasons for this, including the general problems posed by "incomplete information, bounded rationality, inaccurate and biased references, [and] organizational inertia," as well as by problems intrinsic to the jihadist milieu (and, for that matter, certain other extremist milieus), above all ideological fanaticism and religious fatalism.[37] As a result, individual members and entire jihadist cells often ended up learning the wrong lessons or adopting inferior practices.[38] Kenney's findings, which will be echoed and further reinforced in the course of this monograph, should serve as a useful corrective to the claims of a host of security officials, policymakers, and scholars—many with a vested professional interest in exaggerating the jihadist threat[39]—who have long tended to ascribe hyper-rationality, overly coherent strategic thinking, and preternatural levels of operational efficiency to al-Qa'ida and other jihadist terrorist groups.

What is the relevance of all this, especially to the problem of IED fabrication? There is currently an ongoing debate among both scholars and security professionals concerning the degree of difficulty that is purportedly involved in the planning and carrying out of terrorist attacks. Although most experts agree that manufacturing complex explosive devices and launching more sophisticated attacks both require greater preparation and impose higher intrinsic "information costs," some have argued that those same costs for plotting and committing simpler terrorist attacks are relatively low, especially in connection with actions like simple shootings and crude bombings.[40] Others, however, argue that even the successful perpetration of more rudimentary terrorist attacks requires the prior acquisition of a significant amount of *mētis*, a fact that is generally not acknowledged by those emphasizing the low information costs of terrorism.[41] According to Kenney, *mētis*—almost by definition—"imposes substantial information costs on practitioners."[42] After all, even shooting firearms accurately requires a considerable period of prior practice at some sort of firing range—it is not something that can be mastered simply by following written instructions. It follows, then, that carrying out more complicated actions and operations requires even more *mētis*, which in return requires more sustained and/or intensive practice, since developing a real knack for something requires "learning-by-doing."[43]

This is why information about building explosive devices found on the Internet, which is in the form of *techne*, cannot normally substitute for the acquisition of *mētis*, which normally involves obtaining hands-on bomb-making training from experts, followed by frequent practicing of the lessons learned. Even so, the fabrication of sophisticated and destructive IEDs typically requires a combination of *techne* and *mētis*, as Kenney explains:

> Abstract technical knowledge, as found in codified bomb-making recipes, is essential because it contains precise measurements for combining different, often volatile chemicals in precise ways to produce the desired compounds. To be useful, this technical knowledge must be clearly expressed in coherent, step-by-step instructions that readers can follow. However, even when bomb-making recipes are accurate and reliable, which often times they are not, applying this abstract knowledge to meet local needs and circumstances requires practice, the act of assembling bombs from different artifacts with one's own hands, repeatedly. With practice, bomb-makers develop the ability to combine abstract know-what with experimental know-how. This intuitive blending of the abstract with the concrete forms the cornerstone of real world expertise. In this sense, terrorist *techne* and terrorist *mētis* are complimentary, not mutually exclusive.[44]

Although it might not be impossible to construct an explosive device by carefully following instructions found on the Internet, it could be very risky to do so. First, even if the online recipe turns out to be accurate, it can be extremely dangerous to try to mix chemicals or attach detonators without having practiced these activities for a considerable period. Second, it turns out that much of the information found in online bomb-making manuals is either incomplete or seriously inaccurate. Indeed, an explosives expert consulted by Kenney who carefully examined several well-known jihadist online manuals claiming to incorporate bomb-making expertise found that much of the information contained therein was "rubbish."[45] Hence terrorists who lack *mētis* are unlikely to be able to build sophisticated bombs.

That is why it is so important for would-be jihadists to obtain first-hand advice or training from veteran terrorists and professional criminals who are trusted members of their social networks before actually planning attacks, fabricating explosive devices, or attacking selected targets. As Kenney notes:

> Veterans facilitate involvement in terrorism by teaching novices [ideological] concepts and values that support political violence, behavioral norms on how to treat fellow militants and outsiders, and tactical know-how for conducting attacks, including how to case targets, build bombs, lay landmines, safeguard operational security, and handle different types of firearms.[46]

Indeed, experienced militants who had previously received hands-on training overseas and/or seasoned criminals played a vital role in many of the plots and attacks that have been launched by jihadists in Europe.[47] Whether informally or formally, veteran *mujahidin* tended to mingle with, radicalize, recruit, indoctrinate, and eventually — with the help of certain predominantly Muslim petty criminals — transmit technical and operational *mētis* to select would-be jihadists in various locales, including mosques, prisons,

Islamic cultural centers, small shops owned by other "brothers," personal residences, "garage mosques," and at privately-organized study circles, social gatherings, and sporting events.[48]

In any case, the most important indicators of the possible existence of IED *mētis* in this particular context is whether members of various jihadist cells in Europe had received hands-on training from expert bomb makers affiliated with larger, more professional, operationally sophisticated terrorist organizations or, alternatively, whether those cells happened to include, perhaps serendipitously, experienced bomb makers within their own ranks. It is these two questions that will be addressed in Part III of this report, specifically in connection with the devastating March 2004 train bombings in Madrid and the failed July 2006 train bombings near Koblenz and Dortmund.

PART III:

JIHADIST CELLS IN EUROPE AND IED EXPERTISE

The purpose of this section is to examine certain key aspects of two jihadist terrorist plots involving the utilization of improvised explosive devices (IEDs) in Europe, one that was successfully carried out (the 2004 Madrid train bombings) and one that failed (the 2006 Cologne-area train bombings), in an effort to clarify two specific issues: One is the extent to which members of the cells involved in these attacks might have been linked to battle-hardened jihadists and/or operationally sophisticated terrorist organizations or networks elsewhere, from whom they might have obtained some prior hands-on training in bomb making. The other is whether, in lieu of such connections, any members of these cells were themselves experienced bomb makers. The answers to these questions, and the relevance of those answers to the success or failure of the attacks, may in turn help to shed light, at least in a tentative and preliminary fashion, on the following broader issues: First, is it only cells connected to one or more professional terrorist organizations that are likely to be able to carry out (a) devastating single IED attacks and, by extension, (b) sustained "IED campaigns" marked by a succession of such attacks? Two, could these types of IED attacks — or even full-fledged IED campaigns — also be carried out by fully autonomous "self-starter" cells, i.e., cells whose members are inspired by the globally-oriented "jihadist Salafist" ideology espoused by Qa'idat al-Jihad but who are not organizationally or logistically linked in a tangible way to other jihadist networks? Needless to say, the answer to these questions in the European context has significant security implications with respect to IED use and effectiveness for the United States homeland as well.

PRELIMINARY MATTERS

Before turning to the two case studies, however, it is necessary to provide some preliminary information on the different facets of the jihadist threat in Europe, the phases of foreign jihadist implantation in Europe, and the different types of jihadist cells operating there. On the first of these matters, Lorenzo Vidino has justly highlighted the highly variegated nature of the jihadist threat in Europe by drawing a useful distinction between three separate dimensions of that threat. First, there is the "imported" jihadist threat, i.e., that posed by more or less veteran jihadists from Muslim countries who manage to obtain political asylum or guest worker status in European countries but then continue pursuing their extremist aims. Second, there is the "home-brewed" jihadist threat, i.e., that posed by second- and third-generation European Muslims, usually the descendants of foreign immigrant workers, who have become so alienated from and hostile towards their Western homelands that they come to embrace radical forms of Islam and eventually opt to engage in armed jihad. Finally, there is the "home-grown" jihadist threat, i.e., that posed by a small number of European converts to Islam who likewise, as is often the case with "born again" converts, end up embracing extremist doctrines and then go on to join jihadist cells.[49] However valuable these distinctions are, especially in connection with efforts to create a demographic profile of European jihadists, what is most relevant in the context of this monograph is

(1) whether local jihadist cells in Europe were linked organizationally or logistically to veteran jihadist networks in North Africa, the Middle East, or South Asia, and (2) whether any members of those cells, be they imported, home-brewed, or home-grown, had previously received hands-on training in bomb-making from professionals. In short, the question is whether certain members of specific European jihadist cells had managed to develop sufficient levels of *mētis* with respect to IED fabrication.

On the subject of jihadist implantation, one can identify several successive phases.[50] In the first phase, from the late 1970s to the early 1990s, a number of jihadists had flocked to Western Europe in order to obtain political asylum or refugee status and thereby escape persecution at home. Most of these men were either wanted in their own countries for terrorism-related offenses or had not been allowed to return home after fighting in Afghanistan or on other far-flung jihadist fronts, and were thus forced to go elsewhere to establish a new life.[51] For example, many members of the Syrian branch of the Jami'yyat al-Ikhwan al-Muslimin (Society of the Muslim Brothers, better known as the Muslim Brotherhood), an organization which had been brutally suppressed in their Ba'athist-ruled homeland, found refuge in the 1980s in Europe.[52] Although many lay low for a time and focused on rebuilding their personal lives, some soon resurfaced and became actively involved in Islamist activities, including recruiting fighters to go to Bosnia, where during the 1990s Muslims were being subjected to military attacks and reciprocal campaigns of "ethnic cleansing" by Croats and Serbs. Illustrative of such a trajectory was the career of Mustafa Sitt Maryam Nasar (better known as Abu Mus'ab al-Suri), a very important jihadist thinker, operator, and military theorist who resided in several European countries while supporting transnational jihadist activities.[53]

In the second phase, during the mid-1990s, individual jihadists not only began going to Europe to obtain asylum for themselves, but also specifically to establish external support or "rearguard" networks for the terrorist organizations fighting in their home countries, those operating on other jihadist fronts, or for al-Qa'ida.[54] Among the many foreign terrorist groups that such individuals managed to set up support networks for in Europe were al-Jama'a al-Islamiyya (Islamic Group [IG]) and the Tanzim al-Jihad al-Islami (Islamic Jihad Organization[EIJ]) in Egypt; al-Jama'a al-Islamiyya al-Musallaha/Groupe Islamique Armé (Armed Islamic Group [GIA]), the Jaysh al-Islami li-al-Inqadh/Armée Islamique de Salut (AIS: Islamic Salvation Army), and later the Jama'at al-Salafiyya li-al-Da'wa wa al-Qital/Groupe Salafiste pour la Prédication et le Combat (Salafist Group for Preaching and Fighting [GSPC]) in Algeria; the Jabha al-Islamiyya al-Tunisiyya/Front Islamique Tunisien (Tunisian Islamic Front [FIT]), purportedly the military wing of Rashid al-Ghannushi's Hizb al-Nahda (Renaissance Party); the Lajnat al-Difa' 'an al-Huquq al-Shar'iyya (Committee for the Defense of Legitimate [i.e., *shari'a*-based] Rights [CDLR]) in Saudi Arabia; and the Jama'at al-Islamiyya al-Mujahida bi al-Maghrib/ Groupe Islamique Combattant Marocain (Moroccan Islamic Fighting Group [GICM]).[55] Support networks were also created in Western Europe for diverse Bosnian and Chechen jihadist components, and several of the European *mujahidin* who went to fight on those fronts later returned home to promote and wage jihad after having received hands-on training and gaining combat experience.[56]

In the third phase, which began in the latter half of the 1990s and generally continued into the early years of the third millennium, various jihadists began arriving in Europe specifically in order to use the continent as a staging area for planning and carrying out terrorist attacks, either on particular "infidel" Western countries or on Muslim countries ruled by "apostates." To put it another way, there was a shift in jihadist activity inside Europe from a primarily logistical to an increasingly operational role. Many of the individuals involved in this new wave of terrorist operations had previously received hands-on training at al-Qa'ida camps in Afghanistan or at jihadist training camps established in Pakistan, Chechnya, or the Pankisi Gorge region of Georgia.[57] Moreover, most of the plots and attacks they participated in had been secretly instigated or sponsored — and in some cases even devised — by key operational leaders of jihadist groups abroad, including members of al-Qa'ida's *majlis al-shura*, even though these foreign plotters generally left the actual operational details to the designated *'umara* (plural of *'amir*, i.e., commander or prince) of local Europe-based cells. The most important of the externally sponsored attacks that were in part planned and launched by jihadists residing in Europe was the so-called "planes operation" on "blessed Tuesday" (i.e., September 11, 2001 [9/11]),[58] but there were also many other such actions.[59]

In the fourth and final phase, which became more and more pronounced in the wake of the U.S. invasion of Afghanistan and the resulting destruction of al-Qa'ida's Afghan training camp complexes, jihadists in Europe have increasingly resorted to planning and carrying out attacks against the very countries in which they themselves are resident. Indeed, it was in this most recent and still current phase that most of the major terrorist plots and attacks against European countries were launched, including the devastating March 11, 2004, bombings in Madrid and the July 7, 2005, bombings in London.[60] According to some analysts, during this phase there was a shift away from attacks inside Europe that had been sponsored and supported by veteran jihadist groups abroad and towards attacks that were instead planned and carried out by local, fully autonomous cells composed of disgruntled European Muslim citizens or residents who had found a new identity and circle of friends by embracing the "jihadist Salafist" ideology espoused by globally-oriented terrorist networks like al-Qa'ida.[61] In its most extreme formulation, such cells allegedly consisted of amateurish "bunches of guys" who became radicalized, often together in small groups rather than individually, but had no significant logistical or operational linkages to more professional terrorist organizations based outside of Europe. Although in a handful of cases this overly simplistic characterization might be true, in general the actual situation on the ground concerning these cells has been far more complex and murky than such a portrayal indicates, a point that will become clearer in the analysis of the Madrid bombings below.

This debate about the current nature of jihadist cells, both in Europe and elsewhere, has now assumed both a greater degree of salience and a somewhat nasty personal dimension due to the high-profile public dispute between Bruce Hoffman and Marc Sageman. In response to the publication of Sageman's most recent book, *Leaderless Jihad*, which characterizes contemporary jihadist terrorism as primarily a "bottom up" phenomenon, i.e., one in which small local cells are formed by radicalized amateurs on their own initiative, without receiving any direction or tangible support from al-Qa'ida central or other affiliated jihadist terrorist organizations, Hoffman wrote a scathing book review in *Foreign Affairs*.[62] In addition to complaining about Sageman's arrogant dismissal of other terrorism scholarship as well as his displays of historical ignorance and supposedly scientific methodological pretensions, Hoffman argued that al-Qa'ida Central was still a powerful and dangerous organization which not only exerted an inspirational ideological impact, but also still played a significant leadership and operational role in relation to jihadist cells operating in the West.[63] Hence, while not denying that certain localized cells may have formed spontaneously and remained fully autonomous, he rightly emphasized that jihadist terrorism still had a significant "top down" dimension. Similar conclusions had also been reached, both by other scholars and by high-ranking intelligence officials.[64] In his rebuttals in the subsequent issue of *Foreign Affairs* and elsewhere, Sageman insisted that he recognized that the danger posed by al-Qa'ida Central was still substantial, accused Hoffman of mischaracterizing his argument and creating a straw man, and then proceeded to make his own personal attacks.[65]

To some extent this entire back-and-forth polemic has been misleading. First of all, both Sageman and Hoffman recognize that some jihadist terrorist schemes in Europe are effectively "top-down" plots sponsored by al-Qa'ida or other foreign jihadist groups, whereas others are "bottom-up" plots initiated by local, relatively autonomous cells. Hence their real dispute is largely a product of different emphases rather than outright disagreement. As William Mc-

Cants of West Point's Combatting Terrorism Center justly puts it, the "main difference [between them] is over how strong AQ Central is and what relationship it has to those who fight in its name."[66] Second, as noted above, many actual plots have involved a complex combination of top-down and bottom-up features, and in that sense they do not fall squarely into either of these two ostensibly discrete categories.[67] Indeed, in many (if not most) instances, it might be more fruitful to combine these approaches in "ways which provide complementary insights and a deeper level of understanding" instead of articulating them in mutually exclusive forms that "leave little common ground between them."[68] Alas, part of the problem, conceptually speaking, is that the two high-profile analysts and their respective supporters have at times tended to confuse and conflate what are in fact several different types of interactions and interrelationships that have existed between local cells and foreign jihadist organizations. Hence the first desideratum is to distinguish clearly between diverse types of interactions, even though in the real world the situation is typically fluid, dynamic, and therefore messy.

Before actually turning to this question, it is necessary to provide some background information about the basic structure of Qa'idat al-Jihad, the most important of the foreign jihadist organizations that are strongly motivated to carry out terrorist attacks on Western soil. Al-Qa'ida proper is a relatively small organization, numerically speaking, which is divided into two basic levels.[69] First, there are a few dozen members in the so-called *majlis al-shura*, which is internally subdivided into several functionally specialized committees, one of which is concerned explicitly with military affairs.[70] This council effectively constitutes the strategic directorate or officer corps of the group. Second, al-Qa'ida consists of somewhere between several hundred and several thousand rank-and-file members who take their marching orders directly from leading figures of the *majlis al-shura* or their subordinates.[71] These members of the rank-and-file are in turn subdivided into smaller groups known as *anqud* (literally "clusters [of grapes]"), often on a geographic basis that has led, in practice, to clustering on the basis of ethnicity or nationality.[72] That is essentially all there is to al-Qa'ida as an actual organization. If the group's leaders wish to organize an attack themselves, they generally either employ existing members of al-Qa'ida's rank-and-file or recruit suitable volunteers from elsewhere who have already received — or may be currently receiving — training from those rank-and-file members in the group's camps. Alternatively, they may elect to send operatives abroad to radicalize and recruit locals, who then go on to carry out attacks. Strictly speaking, if one was limiting one's analysis to al-Qa'ida Central as an organization, it would only be necessary to consider the actions carried out by its rank-and-file members or those seemingly promising individuals who its leaders had recruited specifically to carry out particular actions, wherever in the world they might be operating.

Unfortunately, there is much more to the Islamist terrorist threat than is represented by the leaders and rank-and-file members of al-Qa'ida's central organization, which is now apparently based somewhere in the Pakistani tribal frontier zone. The issues under consideration here are in fact complicated enormously by two developments. First, al-Qa'ida has established organizational, operational, or logistical affiliations with a host of other Islamist terrorist organizations or factions thereof, both within and outside the Middle East. These affiliated groups and factions have more or less publicly embraced al-Qa'ida's transnational jihadist agenda, including its emphasis on attacking the "far enemy," i.e., the United States and its Western allies. Some of these affiliated organizations have now become quasi-official local branches of al-Qa'ida Central, including the Tanzim Qa'idat al-Jihad fi Bilad al-Rafidayn (al-Qa'ida Organization in Mesopotamia), the Tanzim Qa'idat al-Jihad fi Bilad al-Haramayn (al-Qa'ida Organization in the Land of the Two Holy Places, i.e., the Arabian peninsula), and the Tanzim Qa'idat al-Jihad fi al-Maghrib al-Islami (al-Qa'ida Organization in the Islamic Maghreb), even though they often comprise elements from formerly independent jihadist groups (e.g., in the latter case, the GSPC, the GICM, and similar groups in Tunisia and Libya), whereas others still remain independent groups even though they have adopted the same global jihadist ideology. At the same time, these groups have not entirely abandoned their former local, national, or regional concerns and objectives, much less armed struggles against the "near enemy" in their respective areas. There is no doubt, for example, that self-proclaimed supporters of a global jihad such as factions of Jemaah Islamiyah (Islamic Association [JI]) in Indonesia, the Jaysh Adan-Abyan al-Islami (Aden-Abyan Islamic Army [AAIA]) in Yemen, Lashkar-i Tayyiba and Jaysh-i Muhammad (Army of Muhammad) in Pakistan, the Juma'a Abu Sayyaf (Bearer of Swords Group) in the Philippines, the Fath al-Islam (Conquest of Islam) group in Lebanese refugee camps, and the jihadist "combat *jama'at*s" in the Caucasus are still interested in eventually overthrowing the "infidel" regimes in their own areas or countries, at times even more so than in engaging in global jihad. This should not come as a surprise, since despite his advocacy of a worldwide jihad, Bin Ladin himself had retained a particular interest in destabilizing the Saudi regime in his own homeland, the "Land of the Two Holy Places," and Ayman al-Zawahiri still remains embroiled in Egyptian Islamist infighting despite having left Egypt and opted to merge his own "internationalist" faction of the Tanzim al-Jihad into the al-Qa'ida organization.[73]

Second, as many analysts have argued, in recent years al-Qa'ida has transmogrified from an actual, relatively delimited organization into the organizational expression of a diffuse ideological current that nowadays serves to inspire hundreds of thousands, if not millions, of people across the Muslim world.[74] Although only a small segment of this radicalized population may end up having recourse to terrorism, the result is an ever-growing increase in the threat posed by alleged "self-starter" groups inspired by Bin Ladin's ideology — which some have referred to as "Bin Ladinism" — but that seem at first glance to have few if any tangible organizational, operational, or logistical connections to al-Qa'ida itself. For example, some have argued that the July 7, 2005, London bombings were carried out mainly by small self-starter cells composed of disaffected Muslim citizens or permanent residents who, inspired to respond by the exhortations of al-Qa'ida and other jihadist spokesmen, endeavored to carry out devastating acts of violence against "infidel" Westerners at home.[75] Note that Bin Ladin had always claimed, sometimes disingenuously in an effort to conceal the actual operational involvement of al-Qa'ida, that his primary role was to function as an instigator rather than an actual organizer of jihadist actions.[76] On the other hand, documentary materials recovered from Bin Ladin's hideout in Abbottabad, Pakistan, by the U.S. Navy's Seal Team Six indicate that he was still involved in planning terrorist operations up until his death, and al-Qa'ida Central has reportedly exerted an ever-increasing impact, direct and indirect, on both the ideological and operational characteristics of various Afghan and Pakistani jihadist groups.[77]

However that may be, three European terrorism analysts made an effort in 2007 to distinguish conceptually between three different types of jihadist terrorist operations in Europe. In an article in *Studies in Conflict and Terrorism*, Javier Jordán, Fernando M. Mañas, and Nicola Horsburgh differentiate between what they refer to as: 1) *hit squads*, members of foreign Global Jihad Movement (GJMV) terrorist organizations—like al-Qa'ida, the GSPC, the GICM, or the Jama'at al-Tawhid wa al-Jihad (Unity of God and Jihad Group) network established by Abu Mus'ab al-Zarqawi prior to his June 2006 death in Iraq—who enter Europe from abroad in order to carry out attacks; 2) *local cells* belonging to al-Qa'ida or other foreign terrorist groups which are "autonomous at [the] tactical level" but part of a wider hierarchical organization at [the] strategic and operational levels"; and 3) *grassroots jihadist networks* (GJN), groups of individuals who "accept the strategic objectives of the Global Jihad Movement and attempt to contribute to these from their country of residence" but "do not belong formally to the hierarchical structure" of al-Qa'ida or other GJMV groups.[78] Nevertheless, there are arguably problems with this clear-cut categorization scheme inasmuch as some of these so-called "grassroots networks" have included individuals who were actually members of foreign GJMV groups and might have still been acting at the behest of those groups even if they were no longer in regular contact with or taking direct orders from them. Under these circumstances, it may be misleading to draw such a sharp separation between supposedly "grassroots networks" and bona fide "local cells" established in Western countries by foreign organizations. Very often, in fact, it remains unclear exactly where particular cells fall along this porous and sometimes shifting boundary between Jordán *et al.'s* second and third categories.

Indeed, in order to capture the full complexity of the situation on the ground, it is arguably necessary to make further refinements to the tripartite scheme delineated above. In that spirit, I propose the following categorization system, which expands considerably upon the aforementioned scheme.

1. *Jihadist "hit teams" sent from abroad.*
   - jihadist "hit teams" sent to Europe from elsewhere by al-Qa'ida Central, usually after having been provided with specialized instruction in training camps abroad (perhaps including bomb-making skills), in order to launch terrorist operations and attacks themselves;
   - jihadist "hit teams" sent to Europe from elsewhere by al-Qa'ida's nominal or de facto regional affiliates, perhaps after obtaining specialized training in their respective countries, in order to carry out terrorist operations and attacks themselves;
   - jihadist "hit teams" sent to Europe from elsewhere by other veteran jihadist organizations, perhaps after obtaining specialized training in their respective countries, in order to carry out terrorist operations and attacks themselves.

2. *"Local" jihadist cells organized, supported, and/or directed from abroad.*

- "local" jihadist cells recruited and trained by al-Qa'ida operatives implanted in Europe for that very purpose, and thereafter receiving periodic assistance of various types from al-Qa'ida Central or its regional affiliates;
- "local" jihadist cells recruited and trained by operatives sent by other veteran jihadist groups who were implanted in Europe, sometimes for that very purpose, and thereafter receiving periodic assistance of various types from their parent organizations.

3. *Connected "self-generating" European jihadist cells.*

- "self-generating" European jihadist cells that are in *direct* contact with operatives from al-Qa'ida Central;
- "self-generating" European jihadist cells that are in *direct* contact with operatives from al-Qa'ida's regional affiliates;
- "self-generating" European jihadist cells that are in *direct* contact with operatives from other veteran jihadist groups;
- "self-generating" European jihadist cells that are connected *indirectly*, via intermediaries, to operatives from al-Qa'ida Central, its regional affiliates, or other veteran jihadist groups;
- "self-generating" European jihadist cells that are in *direct* contact with operatives from other European "self-generating" cells;
- "self-generating" European jihadist cells that are connected *indirectly*, via intermediaries, to operatives from other European "self-generating" cells;

- "self-generating" European jihadist cells that include individuals who are members of al-Qa'ida or other foreign terrorist networks.

4. *Isolated or fully autonomous "self-generating" European jihadist cells* that are not connected in any way to members of any other jihadist groups or cells.

This particular system, though perhaps overly elaborate, does permit subtler and more important distinctions to be made than the simpler tripartite scheme proposed by Jordán *et al.*

Nevertheless, a few additional points need to be highlighted. First, one of the problems surrounding the current debate about the nature of jihadist cells in Europe is that arguments are often framed in such a way as to suggest that those cells are either linked to and receiving direction from al-Qa'ida Central itself or, alternatively, that they are fully autonomous. However, neither of these contrasting interpretations, which lie on opposite poles of a much broader spectrum of possible types and levels of interconnectivity or interaction, are necessarily — or even typically — accurate with respect to the situation of really existing European cells. It is crucially important to determine, for example, whether such cells are connected to al-Qa'ida Central or instead, say, to other foreign jihadist groups. Second, the categorization system outlined above is somewhat artificial inasmuch as not all of the enumerated categories are necessarily discrete, much less mutually exclusive. For example, some European cells could conceivably be connected to al-Qa'ida Central, to its regional affiliates, to other veteran jihadist organizations, and/or to other self-generating cells in Europe — factual questions that can only be answered by carrying out in-depth qualitative research. Indeed, it is undeniable that many local jihadist cells in Europe, whether their members were originally recruited by foreign operatives or whether they were initially self-generating, have in fact been connected, directly or indirectly, to terrorist groups based elsewhere. Conversely, it has rarely been the case that allegedly isolated self-generating jihadist cells made up entirely of amateurish "bunches of guys," a phenomenon whose importance has surely been exaggerated by Sageman and his acolytes, have successfully carried out terrorist attacks in the West, including attacks with IEDs.

Hence the key issue is not so much to assess whether members of these European cells have been connected in various ways to other jihadist "brothers," which has normally been the case thus far, but rather to identify exactly who they were connected to and, perhaps even more importantly, to determine precisely how they were connected to them. This is a task that is often not easy to carry out given the lack of detailed information that is presently in the public domain about particular jihadist plots.[79] In such a complex and potentially confusing context it may thus be useful, before examining two IED case studies, to make some general observations about the Social Network Analysis (SNA) of terrorist organizations and networks, a technique that has recently become very faddish.

A social network can be defined as a social structure, however diffuse it may be, that is made up of nodes that are tied to each other by one or more specific types of interdependency.[80] Broadly speaking, SNA involves the "mapping and measuring of relationships and flows between people, groups, [and] organizations."[81] In essence, this mapping and measuring is based on the tracking of nodes and links (or ties) in networks via visual and mathematical analysis. The key to this process is first determining the "location of actors in the network" and thence, by using various measuring techniques, assessing the "centrality" of the various nodes. There are, however, three different centrality measures: 1) *degree centrality*, or the number of direct connections each node has; 2) *between-ness centrality*, or whether nodes are positioned so that they can play "broker" roles vis-à-vis other nodes and networks; and 3) *closeness centrality*, or which nodes have the shortest paths to other nodes. On the basis of previous SNA analyses, it is now generally believed that shorter network paths are most important, since beyond a certain spatial distance particular nodes can no longer influence each other; that so-called "boundary spanners" on the between-ness centrality scale are more important to the overall network due to the bridging roles they can play; and that apparently peripheral nodes that are connected to other, as yet little known networks, may also be of great importance. In any case, according to the proponents of SNA, this approach can yield a great deal of information about the overall network structure by providing more "insight into the various roles and groupings in a network — who are the connectors, mavens, leaders, bridges, [and] isolates, where are the clusters and who is in them, who is in the core of the network, and who is on the periphery?"[82] Who could disagree, at least in theory?

Alas, just as the proponents of numerous other fashionable and not-so-fashionable theories and methodologies have flooded the terrorism field in the wake of 9/11, both in order to appear more relevant and to obtain access to enlarged counterterrorism funding streams, so too have the practitioners of SNA. As a result, there is an ever-growing stream of studies of diverse terrorist networks based on the application of SNA.[83] Given this mad rush to be on the supposed cutting edge of methodological trends, however, some cautionary notes need to be sounded.

First, no methodological technique, no matter how useful, can substitute for subject matter expertise developed over the course of years of study. One of the things that never ceases to amaze serious scholars who have spent years or even decades doing in-depth qualitative research on extremist and terrorist groups is the abysmal ignorance of those subjects displayed by so many self-styled social science "experts," who tend to be fixated on promoting their pet models and theories or who view certain favored methodologies as some sort of "magic bullet" that can allegedly explain and thereby help to resolve every social problem, not to mention predict future human behavior. These presumptions and claims are largely illusory. Despite the immense progress we have made in understanding the material world by applying (natural) scientific methodologies, the complex drivers of human behavior still remain opaque and even, in many fundamental respects, mysterious.[84] Here we are dealing with a fundamental methodological divide within the "social sciences" or, to be more precise, between the "social sciences" and the "humanities." The primary division is between the "social scientists," those who believe that human behavior can best be investigated using the same techniques and methods that are employed in the natural or physical sciences, above all quantitative methods, and the "humanities scholars," those who believe that these natural science methods are often inherently unsuited to studying and understanding far more intangible but vitally important aspects of human behavior. These are complex philosophical and methodological issues that cannot be elaborated upon further in this context, but it is important to emphasize that not every scholar or terrorism researcher agrees that the best way to understand social phenomena and human behavior is to adopt the current social science emphasis on theory-and model-building, hypothesis testing, and quantification. Indeed, the two contrasting groups identified above even employ terms like "empirical" in radically different ways.

Second, the single-minded emphasis on determining the location and centrality of nodes and links in a given network can be very misleading, since many nodes and links that appear to be "central" from a spatial perspective may in fact play a minor functional role in the network. For example, some nodes that initially appear to be important network "hubs" may not turn out to be important at all. Suppose one was doing a "traffic analysis" of communications between purported members of a terrorist group, and one individual appeared to be making and receiving an unusual number of calls every Wednesday night. Without actually monitoring the contents of those phone conversations, there would be no way of knowing whether that individual was performing a vital function such as providing operational instructions to cell members, or whether he was the designated "food man" who was entrusted with calling several "brothers" to find out what they wanted to eat that evening before contacting a restaurant and placing their orders. Indeed, it is not so much the location of such network nodes but rather *the functions that they actually perform for the network* that are of decisive importance. In the context of terrorist networks, then, one should not confuse apparent network "centrality" with operational significance.

Third, the only way to collect and evaluate the massive quantities of factual information that are needed to be able to accurately map a social network is to carry out in-depth qualitative research by systematically consulting a wide array of available primary sources. Based on the principle of "garbage in, garbage out," any SNA mapping or measuring that is based upon seriously incomplete, inaccurate, or otherwise flawed sources of information is virtually guaranteed to be more misleading than illuminating, and thus potentially more harmful than beneficial to those acting on that information. In that sense, the cavalier display of complex diagrams with dozens of crisscrossing lines that purportedly indicate that certain people are linked in some way to others, absent any attempt to clarify the precise nature of those visually depicted links, is all too often confusing rather than enlightening. The hip bone may indeed be connected to the thigh bone, but what function does it actually perform within the skeletal system?

THE 3/11 MADRID TRAIN BOMBINGS

On the morning of March 11, 2004 (3/11), several members of a jihadist cell entered various train cars passing through the so-called "corridor of Henares," i.e., a portion of the Red Nacional de Ferrocarriles Españoles (National Network of Spanish Railways [RENFE]) commuter train system in Madrid situated between the stations of Atocha-Madrid and Alcalá de Henares, where—before exiting from the trains—they deposited backpacks or sports bags filled with a gelatinous nitroglycol-based Spanish-made high explosive known as Goma-2 ECO, nails and screws to produce shrapnel, and industrial electric detonators connected by wires to cell phones. Between 7:37 and 7:40 a.m., someone then detonated 10 of the 13 devices they had left on the trains by means of cell phone signals, killing 191 people and injuring another 1,824, many of them very seriously.

The grim details are as follows.[85] Four bombs were placed on Train 21431, which had stopped to let passengers in and out at the Atocha station: The first exploded on car six at 7:37, the second on car five at 7:38, and the third on car four only 4 seconds later. The bomb in car one fortunately failed to explode and was found later; a squad from the Unidad de Técnicos en Desactivación de Explosivas (Technicians' Unit for Deactivating Explosives [TEDAX]), the bomb disposal specialists from the Cuerpo Nacional de Policía (National Police Corps [CNP]) and the Guardia Civil (Civil Guard [GC]) paramilitary police, then attempted to deactivate it, but it was instead destroyed in a controlled explosion at 9:59 a.m. Four bombs were also placed on Train 21435, which was just leaving the El Pozo del Tío Raimundo station. Two exploded on the upper levels of cars four and five at 7:38, but two others that had been deposited in the lower levels of cars two and three were later found intact. One was detonated on the station platform some time after 9 a.m. that same day in a controlled fashion by TEDAX, whereas the other was inadvertently brought to the police station in the Puente de Vallecas district, where it was discovered the following day and then dismantled in Azorín de Vallecas Park. Meanwhile, one bomb was placed in car four of Train 21713, which was stopped at the Santa Eugenia station, where it too exploded at 7:38. Finally, four bombs were placed on Train 17305, which was then 800 meters from the Atocha station parallel to the Calle Téllez rail line. These bombs (like those on Train 21431) had also been placed in cars one, four, five, and six, and all four exploded at 7:39.

Fortunately, the members of the terrorist cell had made numerous errors in tradecraft that enabled the Spanish police to track them down quickly. For example, three of the bombers had entered the train station at Alcalá de Henares after parking a white Renault Kangoo van in a parking lot on Calle Infantado de Alcalá. An alert doorman named Luis Garrudo who had spotted them called the police after learning of the bombings, and following a cautious but brief on-site investigation the responding officers from Madrid's Brigada Provincial de Información (Provincial Intelligence Brigade [BPI], i.e., anti-terrorism specialists) and the Policía Científica (Forensic Police, i.e., technical specialists) from the Alcalá de Henares police station impounded the van. After a decision was made to transport it to the police station in the Canillas district at 3:30 p.m., the forensic police discovered crucial clues inside the abandoned vehicle, which was owned by José Garzón Gómez but had been stolen in front of his house on Calle Aranjuez on the evening of February 27-28. Among other items, they found seven unused detonators manufactured by the Union Esplosivos Ensign Bickford in a blue plastic trash bag under the passenger seat (similar to those found in the unexploded bombs and various sites linked to the bombers[86]), DNA evidence linking several cell members to the vehicle, and a cassette tape with Arabic-language inscriptions in the glove compartment containing recordings of passages from *sura* 3 (*al-'Imran*: The Family of Amran) of the *Qur'an* that justified the killing of "infidels."[87]

51

However, the bomb found intact in a blue sports bag that had been dismantled in Azorín Park was the single most important of the clues left behind by the perpetrators, since it provided the police with vital forensic details concerning the bombs. That particular device consisted of just over 10 kilograms (kg) of a white, jelly-like explosive (Goma-2 ECO), 640 screws and nails, one detonator marked "made in Spain," copper wires connected to a Mitsubishi Trium T-110 mobile phone, and an MA-0501 cell phone charger.[88] Perhaps more importantly, the Amena SIM card in the mobile phone was soon traced to a batch of 30 sold on February 25, 2008, by Sindhu Enterprise to Jawal Mundo Telecom, located at the Siglo Nuevo shop at Calle Tribulete 17 in the Lavapiés neighborhood, which was owned by the Moroccan Jamal Zugham, one of the key terrorist cell members. It was then determined that 17 of these 30 SIM cards were later activated: 14 of them were used by members of the cell or their associates to make calls, whereas seven were thereafter inserted into 7 Trium T-110 mobile phones, 10 of which had been purchased in early March from the Bazar Top store in Avenida Real de Pinto 42.[89] Those seven SIM cards were turned on the night before the bombings in a small makeshift house in Chinchón on the outskirts of Madrid—where the explosive devices had actually been fabricated—and then utilized on March 11 to receive signals to detonate the bombs.[90] By tracing the seller, buyer, and users of this batch of SIM cards and the phones they were placed in, the police were soon able to attribute the bombings definitively to Islamists, abandon the unlikely Euskadi ta Askatasuna (Basque Fatherland and Freedom [ETA]) trail that was then being publicly promoted by the conservative Partido Popular (People's Party [PP]) government, and rapidly identify several of the actual terrorists.

The Islamist provenance of the bombings was soon after "officially" confirmed, when at 7:38 p.m. on March 13, a call was made by a man speaking Spanish with an Arabic accent to the Telemadrid TV channel, which informed them that a video cassette tape had been deposited in a trash container near the M-30 mosque, one of the largest Islamic mosques in Europe (and, not coincidentally, the locale where Imad al-Din Barakat Yarkas and his associates had previously recruited several worshippers into the al-Qa'ida network in Spain, together with several other individuals who were thence sent to wage jihad on various foreign fronts). When the Panasonic mini-video tape was retrieved from the trash container, wrapped in a blue silk glove and marked "very important" by hand, it turned out to be a video claiming responsibility for the 3/11 attacks.[91] On the video was a man dressed in white with his face covered, wearing a hat, and carrying a machine pistol, standing in front of a green banner with an Arabic inscription of the *shahada* (the profession of Muslim faith, viz., "There is no God but Allah, and Muhammad is His Prophet"), who identified himself as Abu Dujan[a] al-Afghani, the spokesman for the military wing of Ansar al-Qa'ida fi Urubba (The Partisans of al-Qa'ida in Europe).[92] The individual reading this message was later identified as a Moroccan born in Tetuan named Rashid Awlad, who then read out a message in classical Arabic claiming that the bombings were carried out in response to Spain's participation in the war being waged against Islam by "international terrorist organizations" headed by U.S. President George W. Bush and his followers, and warned that more bloody attacks were to come unless Spain ceased its "killings" of and "injustices" against Muslims. He reiterated the standard jihadist rhetoric to the effect that the *mujahidin* would keep fighting until they achieved victory or martyrdom because they loved death more than the nonbelievers loved life, and concluded by reading a verse from the *Qur'an*.[93] This video was followed up by two more jihadist claims of responsibility, one from the Kata'ib Abu Hafs al-Masri (Abu Hafs al-Masri Brigades) that was faxed to *al-Hayat* and emailed to *al-Quds al-'Arabi*, two London-based Arab newspapers, on March 15, and another that was faxed on April 3 at 6:05 p.m. to the Spanish newsweekly *ABC* and signed by Abu Dujan al-Afghani on behalf of the so-called Death Brigade (Brigada de la Muerte, probably Katiba al-Qatl in Arabic) of Ansar al-Qa'ida in Europe, which reiterated his previous threats.[94]

In any case, it turned out that Zugham himself was already well known to investigators from both the Unidad Central de Información Exterior (Central Unit for Foreign Intelligence [UCIE]) and the Centro Superior de Información de la Defensa (Higher Center for Defense Intelligence [CESID]), two security services that had been closely monitoring Islamist activists in Spain since 1995.[95] Not only was he a member of Imad al-Din Barakat Yarkas' al-Qa'ida network in Spain, one of the largest and most important in Europe, he was also a personal friend and confidant of Barakat Yarkas (better known as Abu Dahdah). Indeed, in response to a request from French anti-terrorist magistrate Jean-Louis Bruguière in the summer of 2001, the police had surreptitiously entered Zugham's flat and found important material related to jihadist activities. Later on, his name surfaced in connection with the investigation of the May 16, 2003, bombings in Casablanca, five suicide attacks carried out by jihadists linked to the GICM. Moreover, both real and would-be jihadists had used his Siglo Nuevo store on a regular basis to make calls home to Morocco or to other countries, and he had long been intimately associated with a close-knit network of jihadist sympathizers in Lavapiés. Once his name surfaced in connection with the SIM card purchases, Zugham and two employees in his shop were quickly arrested in the late afternoon on March 13, only 2 days after the attacks.[96]

On March 16, another key trail was uncovered.[97] After tracing more of the calls made from the mobile phones with the SIM cards and their locations at the time, agents from the Unidad Central de Apoyo Operativo (Central Operational Support Unit [UCAO]) who were working at the behest of the UCIE determined that a March 4 call had been made by a cell member from a phone booth in Avilés to the home of Carmen María Toro Castro, the wife of a 27-year-old former miner named José Emilio Suárez Trashorras. Suárez Trashorras was a petty criminal who, after having been arrested for possession of drugs, Goma-2 explosives, and 94 detonators in "Operación Pipol," had been recruited in July 2001 as a confidential informant by Manuel García Rodríguez (nicknamed Manolón), a police officer who had previously worked for an anti-terrorist unit but had then become head of the Brigada de Estupefacientes (Illicit Drug Squad) in the Avilés police station. Over the years Suárez Trashorras had then provided certain inside information that had led to the arrest of other petty criminals for drug trafficking. Indeed, right after the 3/11 attacks, Suárez Trashorras told Manolón that it had been the "Moors," not ETA, who were responsible. This was confirmed after a March 17 phone conversation between Rafa Zuhayr, a Moroccan petty criminal and confidential informant of the GC, and a member of the GC's Unidad Central Operativa (Central Operational Unit [UCO]) named Víctor—a conversation monitored by the Madrid anti-drug police—revealed vital details about a key individual involved in the 3/11 attacks, Jamal Ahmidan (nicknamed "El Chino," i.e., "the Chinaman").[98] This small lead eventually enabled the police to reconstruct the activities of a group of radicalized Moroccan criminals who obtained the explosive materials and detonators from some Spanish counterparts in Asturias in exchange for drugs and then arranged for them to be transported to the house in Chinchón, where the members of the operational cell used them to fabricate the bombs.

On March 22, officers from the UCAO finally located that small house in Chinchón, which was situated not far from Alcalá de Henares, at kilometer 14 on Road 313, which links Morata de Tajuña and Titulcia.[99] After keeping it under surveillance for 3 days, the police broke down the door and entered the domicile on March 25, where they found residues of nitroglycol and ammonium nitrate, two components of dynamite; materials from detonators; 105 cartridges; DNA traces from several cell members; and other important forensic evidence.[100] It turned out that Ahmidan had rented the ramshackle property on January 18 under the false name of Yusuf ibn Salah, and that it had subsequently been used to hold meetings, store explosives and detonators, and construct the actual bombs.[101] By then, the police had correctly identified key figures in the two main components of the 3/11 cell, Ahmidan and Zugham, and it was only a matter of locating and arresting Ahmidan and the other remaining members of the group before they succeeded in carrying out further bloody attacks. This became all the more imperative on April 2, when a bomb similar to those used in the 3/11 train car attacks was found alongside the tracks of the Alta Velocidad Española (AVE: Spanish High Speed) train line between Madrid and Seville, in the Mocejón zone near Toledo. Apparently, the device had been placed there between 7:20 and 10 a.m. that morning, and contained 12 kilograms of Goma-2 ECO and an electric detonator attached to a long-distance 136 meter cable, but no attached battery or cell that could be used to ignite the detonator.[102]

Meanwhile, after following several more leads and arresting a few other cell members, on April 3 the UCAO tracked several of the key remaining plotters to a first floor apartment at Calle de Martín Gaite 40 in the Leganés district in southern Madrid. By tracing and monitoring certain mobile phones in which the SIM cards of interest had been inserted, including that of Rashid Awlad, they learned that this particular apartment had been rented on March 8 by a Moroccan GICM leader named Yusuf ibn al-Hajj. At around 4 p.m., a couple of dozen policemen converged on the apartment building, and one of them then rang the bell of the targeted apartment on a bogus pretext in order to determine whether persons with Arab accents were residing there.[103] This brief interchange on the intercom raised the suspicions of the occupants, who sent a trained sprinter named 'Abd al-Majid Abu Shar downstairs to check out the situation. When Abu Shar saw the police, he immediately ran off at full speed but apparently also managed to alert his colleagues upstairs, one of whom suddenly appeared on the porch of the apartment and fired machine gun bursts at a group of policemen below. As a result, between 5:30 and 6:30 p.m. heavily-armed anti-terrorist police from the Grupo Especial de Operaciones (Special Operations Group [GEO]) arrived on the scene and, together with dozens of other policemen and intelligence officers, established a security cordon around the building as well as a field hospital and listening posts. From inside the apartment, voices and chanting in Arabic could be heard, which fueled concerns that the occupants might suddenly charge out of the apartment with explosive vests on and blow themselves up. Efforts by the GEO to initiate negotiations commenced around 8 p.m., but in response the terrorists simply threatened to blow up the building. At 8:30, several GEO men ascended the stairs, blew open the door, and fired smoke canisters into the apartment, but the inhabitants still refused to come out. Instead, they made several phone calls to loved ones or other "brothers." Finally, at 9:03 p.m. the terrorists sat down in a circle together and detonated a huge explosion, destroying a substantial part of the building, "martyring" themselves, and killing a GEO officer named Francisco Javier Torronteras. In the ruins of the apartment, the Forensic Police found much vitally important evidence, including the body parts of seven cell members, 236 detonators, 30 kilograms of Goma-2 ECO, four machine pistols, jihadist written and audio materials, plans prepared for the carrying out of future terrorist attacks, and a videotape of three of the cell members transmitting a belligerent message to the Spaniards about their motivations and future plans.[104]

This siege was the most dramatic event that occurred during the actual search for the terrorist bombers. After the death of most of the material perpetrators at Leganés, the police followed additional evidentiary trails, examined residences in various locales which the cell members had rented, and arrested several other individuals who were implicated in the plot, including the remaining Spanish petty criminals in Asturias who had provided the explosive materials and detonators to the jihadists. Meanwhile, the lengthy judicial investigations and proceedings began which eventually culminated in the controversial verdict that was issued in 2007.

Links Between 3/11 Cell Members and Other Jihadist Organizations.

Many knowledgeable observers of the jihadist milieu, above all within Europe, were astounded when Judge Javier Gómez Bermúdez issued the court's final verdict concerning the Madrid train bombings on October 31, 2007. For one thing, many of the defendants got off with very light sentences, to the chagrin of members of the 11-M Asociación Afectados de Terrorismo (Association of Persons Affected by 3/11 Terrorism) and most other victims' associations.[105] For another, the court severely punished various "small fry," including some of the petty criminals who had procured the explosives and detonators, but ended up dropping the most serious charges against certain "bigger fish" in the jihadist milieu who were arguably far more responsible for instigating, encouraging, and perhaps even helping to plan the operation.[106] As noted above, most of the actual bomb placers blew themselves up when the police surrounded their apartment in Leganés, which prevented them from being arrested and prosecuted for their crimes. Hence it was incumbent upon the court to uncover and prosecute some of the instigators and planners behind the attacks, a task they arguably failed to perform adequately, especially given the damning information gathered in the course of the investigation that was reflected in the initial indictment and thence informed the public prosecutor's written statement. Even granting that various peculiarities of the Spanish judicial system may have made it difficult to prosecute those who were not material perpetrators or more advisable not to do so in order to forestall endless appeals, it is difficult to understand why the attacks were characterized as being "without intellectual authors" or why the serious charges against key al-Qa'ida- or GICM-linked figures such as Rabi' 'Uthman al-Sayyid Ahmad (alias "Muhammad al-Masri [the Egyptian]") and 'Amir al-'Azizi ended up being dropped altogether or reduced to lesser charges.

Long before the final verdict was issued, there had been an ongoing debate among terrorism analysts concerning the extent to which the 3/11 terrorist cell was autonomous or, alternatively, whether it was linked to and operating at the behest of foreign terrorist organizations. Perhaps not surprisingly, attitudes on this issue were generally influenced by whether those analysts already viewed al-Qa'ida primarily as an organization, however networked, horizontal, diffuse, and "franchised" it might have been, and those who viewed it essentially as the high-profile vanguard and self-proclaimed mouthpiece of a much broader "social movement." Those in the former camp were more apt to view the Madrid bombings as an action sponsored or at least supported in some way by al-Qa'ida and/or its affiliates, whereas those in the latter camp were prone to view the 3/11 cell as a self-generating and rather amateurish group of friends and kinsmen who, though inspired by al-Qa'ida's global jihadist ideology, undertook violent actions on their own initiative without any meaningful assistance from al-Qa'ida itself or from other professional terrorist organizations.[107] Similarly, the former generally viewed the October 2007 3/11 trial verdict as severely problematic, if not as a miscarriage of justice, whereas the latter tended to see it as a belated legal confirmation of their own prior perspective.[108] Unfortunately, a good deal of this debate has missed the point inasmuch as it has grossly oversimplified, if not inadvertently mischaracterized, the diverse and complex nature of the links that have often existed in the past—and are perhaps also likely to exist in the future—between al-Qa'ida and local jihadist cells. Before offering further thoughts on this matter, however, it is necessary to survey the historical development and identify the functional components of the 3/11 cell.

According to the public prosecutor, high-ranking policemen, attorneys representing the relatives of the victims, and certain independent journalistic or academic investigators, the cell responsible for the Madrid bombings had two main components.[109] The first was the operational group that actually carried out the bomb attacks, which was composed of Sirhan ibn 'Abd al-Majid Fakhit (nicknamed "the Tunisian"), Zugham, Jamal Ahmidan, Rashid Awlad, his brother Muhammad Awlad, 'Abd al-Nabi' Kunja'a, Anwar Asrih Rifa'at, and 'Ali Kamal al-Amari, as well as their direct helpers, such as Da'ud Awnani, Abu Shar, and Muhammad al-Falah.[110] The second was the logistical support group that procured the explosives and detonators used in the attacks as well as providing other necessary resources and services, such as financing (derived largely from illicit activities like theft, fraud, and drug trafficking), false documents, stolen cars, safe houses, etc. This group consisted of actual jihadist cell members like Jamal Ahmidan, 'Uthman al-Ghanawi, Rashid Akhlif, and 'Abd al-Ilah al-Fadl al-Akil, as well as other petty criminals who worked with them but were seemingly unaware of the scope and/or details of the planned attacks, such as Hamid Ahmidan, Nasr al-Din Abu Sabah, Mahmud Sulayman A'un, and Rafa Zuhayr.[111] Note that Jamal Ahmidan participated in both of these types of activities, and was thus a key liaison man between the operational and logistical support groups, whereas Zuhayr was the individual who brought Jamal into contact with the Spanish petty criminals in Asturias who provided the cell with Goma-2 ECO and industrial detonators that they had pilfered from a mine. Having identified the principal culprits, the next desideratum is to discuss the backgrounds of some of these individuals in order to demonstrate that the 3/11 terrorist cell does not conform to the widely disseminated notion, peddled by Atran and Sageman, that it was a "self-generating" group of amateurs without significant connections to al-Qa'ida or other jihadist organizations.

Beginning with the operational group members, the first point that needs to be emphasized is that the two key personnel in that group—Fakhit and Zugham—were previously members of Abu Dahdah's al-Qa'ida network in Spain.[112] So, too, were eight other individuals who were allegedly involved in the 3/11 plot. These included a purported mastermind of the attack, the Moroccan Sa'id ibn al-Arraj; two men who are believed to have helped inspire or instigate it, the Moroccans 'Amir al-'Azizi (alias 'Uthman al-Andalusi) and Mustafa al-Maymuni; two others who participated in meetings along with cell members where jihad was glorified and/or where preliminary attack plans were hatched, the Moroccans Sa'id al-Shadadi and Idris al-Shabli; and three who performed certain minor tasks in relation to the renting of the house in Chinchón, the Syrians Muhammad

Nidal, Walid al-Taraki al-Masri (despite his appellation "the Egyptian"), and Muhammad Badr al-Din al-Akkad.[113] Al-Maymuni and al-'Azizi were likewise important figures, respectively, in the Moroccan jihadist groups al-Salafiyya al-Jihadiyya (Jihadist Salafism) and the GICM, whose 'amir Nur al-Din Nafi'yya had sworn a personal oath of loyalty (bay'a) to Bin Ladin in 1999 and thereafter formed a pact with al-Qa'ida.[114] Even this cursory summary should serve to cast some doubt on the confident assertions by Atran and Sageman concerning the supposed "self-generating" nature and organizational autonomy of the 3/11 attackers, but as soon as one becomes more familiar with the extensive activities and contacts of Abu Dahdah's earlier network and examines the background of some of these individuals in more detail, such a portrayal appears even more untenable.

As mentioned above, the al-Qa'ida network in Spain was among the most important components of the infrastructure that Bin Ladin's lieutenants had implanted in the European continent.[115] This network first began to coalesce in the early- to mid-1990s under the leadership of a Palestinian militant named Anwar Adnan Muhammad Salih (alias Shaykh Salih) and two former members of the Syrian branch of the Muslim Brotherhood, Abu Dahdah and—in the initial stages—Abu Mus'ab al-Suri.[116] In 1994 Abu Dahdah and Shaykh Salih began actively peddling the radical global jihadist ideas of 'Umar Mahmud 'Uthman (alias Abu Qatada)—who is generally regarded as al-Qa'ida's "spiritual leader" in Europe—at the Abu Bakr mosque, located in Madrid's Tetuan neighborhood at Calle Anastasio Herrero 7, in order to spot and vet suitable worshippers there for induction into a radical grouping known as the Alianza Islámica (Islamic Alliance, probably al-Hilf al-Islami in Arabic). The youngest and most radical members of that group were thence recruited into an even more militant, secretive, and activist group known as the Soldados de Alá (Soldiers of Allah, Jund Allah in Arabic), which thereafter became the core of al-Qa'ida's network in Spain. Several members of the Soldados, along with other likely candidates, were then recruited and sent to fight on various jihadist fronts abroad, in particular Bosnia and Chechnya.

This situation persisted until October 1995 when, at the orders of al-Qa'ida's Saudi logistics chief Zayn al-Abidin Muhammad Husayn (alias Abu Zubayda), Shaykh Salih departed for Peshawar to manage the local office of Bin Ladin's Maktab al-Khidamat li al-Mujahidin (MAK: Services Bureau for the Mujahidin), leaving Abu Dahdah in charge of the Spanish network. The latter continued his work of recruiting *mujahidin* and, with the help of Shaykh Salih and Abu Zubayda, arranging for their logistical needs, e.g., the provision of documents, transportation to camps in Afghanistan for training, sustenance, equipping with weapons, and eventual transit to jihadist battlefields where Muslims were in open conflict with non-Muslims.[117] However, a schism developed within the Soldados when a puritanical fanatic named 'Abd Allah Khayat Kattan (alias Abu Ibrahim) joined the group, which was then engaged in proselytizing at the Centro Islámico de Madrid inside the huge M-30 mosque, and decided to challenge the leadership of Abu Dahdah. The bitter infighting between the two factions within the organization abruptly ended in 1997 when Abu Ibrahim left Spain and went to Jordan, thereby leaving Abu Dahdah as its sole leader.

Apart from being actively engaged for years in indoctrinating and radicalizing alienated Muslims in Spain, recruiting and training suitable candidates to go abroad and wage jihad on various fronts, and providing medical care and refuge for returning jihadist veterans, another noteworthy feature of the Abu Dahdah network was that its key personnel maintained extensive ongoing interactions with "fraternal" al-Qa'ida branches and affiliated jihadist networks, both in other European countries and abroad.[118] Indeed, it was largely because of this elaborate spider web of personal and organizational connections which they had nurtured that Abu Dahdah and his lieutenants were able to perform their vital recruitment and logistical services for the global jihadist cause. Among the numerous groups that Alianza Islámica personnel regularly interacted with were al-Qa'ida branches in Britain (through Abu Qatada, Abu Mus'ab al-Suri, and Khalid al-Fawaz of the CDLR), Germany (through Ma'mun Darkazanli and Muhammad Haydar Zammar, two Syrian Muslim Brotherhood members, and the Moroccan Sa'id bin al-Hajji, all three of whom were linked to the 9/11 plotters), and Italy (through Muhammad the Egyptian), as well as groups such as the Algerian Jabha al-Islamiyya li al-Inqadh/Front Islamique du Salut (Islamic Salvation Front [FIS]) and GIA; the Jama'a al-Muqatila al-Tunisiyya/Groupe Combattant Tunisien (Tunisian Fighting Group [GCT]), the military wing of the FIT (through Tariq Ma'arufi in Belgium); the Kurdish Islamist group Ansar al-Islam (Partisans of Islam) through Shaykh Mahar; jihadist organizations in the Balkans and Chechnya; and many others.

Of most interest to American readers, of course, is the fact that individuals connected to the Abu Dahdah network were apparently aware of and may have helped to facilitate the 2001 visits of Muhammad 'Ata' and Ramzi bin al-Shayb to Spain. Between July 9 and July 16 of that year, the two 9/11 conspirators met near the city of Tarragona to discuss further operational details and potential pitfalls concerning the forthcoming "planes operation," details that were subsequently transmitted by al-Shayb to al-Qa'ida Central.[119] Al-Shayb likewise flew to Madrid on September 5 and rented a room for 2 days prior to flying to Dubai via Athens on September 7. According to the Spanish indictment, four members of the Abu Dahdah network may have provided cover and support for these activities—the Algerian Muhammad ibn al-Fatmi, al-Shabli, al-'Azizi, and Abu Dahdah himself.[120] On May 26, al-Fatmi called Abu Dahdah and made several cryptic remarks suggesting that he may have had foreknowledge of major operations to come, such as "the brothers have to hurry" and "you should consign the stuff soon." In June al-Fatmi moved to an apartment in Tarragona, very near to the area where 'Ata' and al-Shayb met the following month, and shortly after those meetings he began making preparations to move to Karachi, where he flew on September 3, along with three other Algerian jihadists linked to the 9/11 cell, including Sa'id bin al-Hajji (whose address book contained Abu Dahdah's old phone number). Furthermore, al-'Azizi's close associate al-Shabli phoned Abu Dahdah on September 5, the same day that al-Shayb arrived in Madrid, and made a comment about "Muhammad the Algerian" (i.e., al-Fatmi) before being cut off by Abu Dahdah, who was concerned that he might make compromising remarks. In the months before 9/11, there were also a series of suggestive phone calls between someone named "Shakur" (the alias of a Moroccan based in the United Kingdom [UK] named

Fakhit Hilali) and Abu Dahdah, in which allusions were seemingly made to the planned hijackings, e.g., one on August 27, 2001, in which Shakur said, "In our lessons, we have entered the field of aviation and have cut the bird's throat."[121] In any event, the role of the Abu Dahdah network in this and other al-Qa'ida operations was considered sufficiently important that, after years of being closely monitored by the Spanish police, its key cadres were arrested in "Operación Dátil" on November 13-14, only 2 months after the 9/11 attacks.

Some remarks must now be made about certain key members of the two components of the 3/11 cell, beginning with individuals in the operational cell who had documented affiliations with other jihadist organizations and networks. The first of these was Fakhit, whose social and educational background was quite elevated in comparison to that of most other members of the cell.[122] Fakhit was born in Tunis in 1968 into a Westernized upper middle class family.[123] His father and mother both worked for the Tunisian foreign ministry, and helped arrange for Fakhit, an outstanding student, to obtain a scholarship administered by the Agencia Española de Cooperación Internacional (Spanish Agency for International Cooperation) so that he could study Economics at the Universidad Autónoma de Madrid. Fakhit arrived in Madrid in 1996 to commence his studies and, thanks to a substantial academic stipend and financial assistance from his family, was able to live very well. When he first arrived, the shy, culturally conservative Tunisian sometimes joined his fellow students in attending discotheques and other "infidel" social outings, but he soon shifted gears and began publicly criticizing Western policies towards Islam, spending more of his free time worshipping at the Saudi-funded M-30 mosque, studying the *Qur'an* intensively there, and becoming increasingly prominent in mosque activities. This enabled him to visit Mecca in 1998, after which he became even more religiously devout. Eventually, Fakhit became an "inflexible Islamist and assiduous orator" at the M-30 mosque.[124] However, he soon began gravitating towards more radical personalities who sought to use the mosque as a recruiting ground, and over time he and his new associates grew increasingly hostile to the relatively moderate Wahhabi imam of the mosque, the Egyptian Mahmud al-Munir.[125]

In 1999 and 2000, Fakhit began attending periodic weekend picnics along the Alberche River with Syrian Islamists Muhannad al-Mallah Dabas and his brother Mu'taz (who was directly connected to Abu Qatada and other al-Qa'ida's leaders in Europe), al-'Azizi, Abu Dahdah, and various mosque-goers, get-togethers where he and these latter attendees were further exposed to jihadist propaganda. The regular members of this group, one of whose leaders was the veteran *mujahid* al-'Azizi, eventually began referring to themselves as the Ikhwan al-Shuhada (Brotherhood of Martyrs). Meanwhile, Fakhit began inviting select mosque-goers to an apartment at Virgen del Coro 14, where Muhannad al-Mallah and other extremists played "atrocity" and pro-jihadist videos in an effort to anger and radicalize them. According to the police, moreover, by 2001 Fakhit had converted his own residence into a "place of lodging and cover for young Muslims undergoing a process of radical conversion," but in exchange the lodgers had to abide by strict Taliban-style regulations against listening to music or watching television.[126] After the 9/11 attacks, Shuhada and al-Qa'ida members openly broke with the imam of the M-30 mosque, who had publicly condemned the devastating attacks that the former instead referred to positively as "white Tuesday," white being the color associated by Muslims with purity. Indeed, they eventually accused al-Munir, in true *takfiri* fashion, of being a "hypocrite" and an "infidel."[127]

After the arrests of Abu Dahdah and his main lieutenants, Fakhit and other less prominent members of the network assumed a low profile for a while before coalescing and resuming their plotting anew. In 2002 the Tunisian joined a new group headed by al-Maymuni that was known as the Harakat al-Salafiyya al-Jihadiyya (Jihadist Salafist Movement).[128] This small group, whose members included al-Maymuni, Fakhit, al-Shabli, Muhammad al-Arbi bin Salam, al-Falah, and others, began holding lengthy regular meetings, both at the residence of Faysal al-'Ush and during excursions to the Alberche River, where intense discussions continued about how, when, and where to best attack the "Crusaders." The most important issue was whether group members should go off to fight on foreign battlefields or instead wage jihad directly against the "infidel" societies where they resided; this latter option was eventually chosen after Spain sent troops to participate in the U.S. invasion of Iraq.[129] Key members of this Salafiyya group then hooked up with another small group of militants that had been formed in Spain by Muhammad the Egyptian, which included the Syrian ex-engineering student Basil Ghalyun, Muhannad and Mu'taz al-Mallah, and a Moroccan student of aeronautical engineering named Fu'ad al-Murabit Amghar.[130] Personnel from these two groups subsequently formed the kernel of the operational component of the 3/11 cell. Last but certainly not least, in the latter half of 2003, in the course of frequenting various Maghribi locales in the Calle Tribulete area in Madrid's Lavapiés district, including the Tanger barbershop (where many cell members collectively drank water that had been blessed and brought from Mecca by its proprietor, 'Abd al-Wahid ibn al-Arraj), the al-Manara *halal* butcher shop, the Alhambra Cafeteria and Restaurant, and Zugham's Siglo Nuevo phone shop, Fakhit developed a close friendship with Jamal Ahmidan.[131] Their growing collaboration soon brought Fakhit's group into the orbit of Ahmidan's own criminal network, which thence provided key logistical support for the 3/11 attacks. In fact, both men were later accused of placing explosive devices inside trains on that tragic day, and both then ended up "martyring" themselves in the Leganés apartment.

Most importantly in this context, Fakhit's transformation into an Islamist extremist was facilitated *personally and directly*, at various stages, by key individuals linked to al-Qa'ida. One of these was Ahmad Ibrahim, a Moroccan whose daughter Nura for a time became Fakhit's fiancée. Ibrahim made his living for over a decade by selling recreational boats in Palma de Mallorca, wore a waist-length beard, and forced both his Finnish wife and their daughter to wear a black *burqa*. He was arrested in 2002 near Barcelona by the GC after Judge Ismael Moreno accused him of being al-Qa'ida's main financial operative in Spain. During several trips to Palma between 2000 and 2002, Fakhit had received personal ideological instruction from Ibrahim.[132] A second important influence in Fakhit's transformation was the Afghan returnee al-'Azizi, who became the leader of the Shuhada group in whose social activities Fakhit regularly participated, and also provided frequent guidance on ideological matters.[133] A third was Abu Dahdah himself, another regular Shuhada group attendee whose network Fakhit later joined, thereby becoming increasingly integrated into that milieu prior to its decapitation and partial dismantling in late 2001.[134] A fourth was al-Maymuni, who also attended or hosted gatherings of the Shuhada group. Fakhit and al-Maymuni, both acolytes of al-'Azizi, later became so close that the Tunisian allowed al-Maymuni's wife Nayat to move into his apartment and married al-Maymuni's daughter Hanani.[135] In 2002, a confidential police informant nicknamed "Cartagena" (who was later identified as 'Abd al-Qadir al-Farsawi, the imam of the al-Taqwa mosque in the Villaverde district in southern Madrid), reported that al-Maymuni had formed and become the leader of the aforementioned Salafiyya group, which included Fakhit. Indeed, when al-Maymuni left Spain in early 2003 in order to organize jihadist cells in Morocco (activities for which he was arrested by the Moroccan authorities in the wake of the May 2003 Casablanca bombings), Fakhit replaced him as the new leader of the group.[136] A fifth was Muhammad the Egyptian. In the wake of the flight from Spain of several important members of al-Qa'ida's European network, including al-'Azizi, Fakhit not only became a de facto leader of remnants of Abu Dahdah's group but also a disciple of the Egyptian's, who had returned to Spain in the summer of 2002.[137] In short, the primary animator of the 3/11 cell had long operated within the orbit of leading al-Qa'ida figures in Spain, who had *personally overseen his ongoing religious, political, and ideological indoctrination and radicalization.* How, then, can anyone seriously argue that the 3/11 cell was a "self-starter" group that had no meaningful connections to al-Qa'ida?

Another important member of the 3/11 operational cell was Jamal Zugham, who as noted above had become a member of the al-Qa'ida network in Spain and a close personal friend of Abu Dahdah's.[138] On March 13, 2003, after the two Indian shopkeepers who had sold the phones and SIM cards to the plotters identified Zugham as the individual who had purchased the latter, investigators from the UCIE immediately became alarmed given that he was already very well-known to the anti-terrorist police.[139] Zugham was born in 1973 in Tangiers, and was the eldest son of the *mu'adhdhin* at the mosque in the city's Shar ibn Dibani neighborhood. In 1985 he arrived in Spain, where he initially found work as a fruit dealer in the San Fernando market on Calle Tribulete. Like many immigrants, he eventually opened up his own small shop, drifted into various semi-licit economic activities, and found it more comforting to associate with other North Africans in Lavapiés, including his relatives and countrymen, than to interact socially with Spaniards. As a result, he ended up befriending several individuals in the area who had joined Abu Dahdah's network, including Sa'id al-Shadadi, or thence found their way into its bastard offspring, the 3/11 cell, such as Rashid Akhlif.[140]

Zugham's increasing involvement in the activities of various components of al-Qa'ida's network in Europe was confirmed on August 10, 2001, when UCIE agents surreptitiously entered and searched his apartment at Calle de Sequillo 14.[141] They did so at the request of French judicial authorities after David Courtailler, a French convert to Islam who joined a jihadist cell that had planned to attack the American embassy in Paris, admitted that he had had a meeting with Zugham in a Madrid mosque in 1998.[142] In the course of that search, the policemen discovered that Zugham possessed the phone number of al-'Azizi. Similarly, in Abu Dahdah's appointment book confiscated during the "Dátil" investigation, Zugham's number was listed under the heading "Jamal from Tangiers." This and several other indicators led investigators to conclude that Zugham functioned as the virtual *dauphin* (heir apparent) of Abu Dahdah.[143] Whether or not that is true, there is no doubt that the former had "extensive international connections with figures involved in some way or another with the jihad," including the Norway-based "spiritual leader" of the Kurdish jihadist group Ansar al-Islam, Najm al-Din Faraj Ahmad (alias Mullah Krikar), and several militants who played important roles in Moroccan jihadist groups.[144] For that very reason, Zugham was subsequently investigated by Judge Garzón in connection with the multiple May 16, 2003, terrorist attacks carried out in Casablanca by a cell from al-Salafiyya al-Jihadiyya, since he was closely linked to a member of that network, 'Abd al-'Aziz ibn Ya'ish, who the Moroccan authorities believed was involved in those bombings and therefore sought to have extradited from Spain. Zugham also was inspired by and had personal interactions with Muhammad al-Fizazi, an extremely radical Moroccan imam who had not only previously exerted a powerful ideological influence on 'Ata' and several future 9/11 hijackers during his stint preaching at the al-Quds (Jerusalem) mosque in Hamburg, but was also widely regarded as one of the spiritual leaders of al-Salafiyya al-Jihadiyya and other terrorist groups in his homeland.[145] Later, in the weeks before the Madrid bombings, Zugham reportedly attended gatherings together with other 3/11 cell members at the Chinchón house.[146] After the attacks, Zugham was

quickly arrested when the SIM card found in the unexploded bomb at the El Pozo station was traced to
the batch purchased by his store. He was subsequently identified by two surviving train passengers as the
individual they had seen leaving a bag on the train car
they were riding in, which then blew up.

A third figure who played a vital role in the 3/11
bombings was Jamal Ahmidan. Although much—
arguably too much—has been made about the poor
slums in Moroccan cities as alleged breeding grounds
of jihadism, Ahmidan was born in 1970 in Tetuan into
a relatively well-off middle class family and had 13
siblings.[147] His father Ahmad had worked in Holland
for several years in order to make his fortune, leaving
his wife at home, but when he returned he had sufficient funds to set up a fabric business and eventually was able to buy a second house on the beach in
Tangiers. He was religious and hoped that his sons
would be inspired by his own example, but Jamal
was always very headstrong, hotheaded, and impul-
sive, and ended up dropping out of high school. Both
he and his elder brother Mustafa loved their mother
Rahma but had a strained relationship with their father, and as a result, both began engaging in drug trafficking rather than following in Ahmad's respectable
footsteps. At first they made money selling Moroccan
hashish directly in Spain, or instead selling it in Holland in exchange for cocaine and MDMA (3,4-methy-
lenedioxymethamphetamine or "ecstasy"), which
they then sold in Spain. In 1991 Jamal followed two
of his brothers to Madrid, but managed to enter Spain
only by falsely claiming to be an Algerian seeking
asylum. After settling in the Spanish capital, he soon
formed his own criminal network that was composed
largely of friends and kinsmen from home. As time

progressed, he expanded the range of his criminal activities, and eventually became involved in car theft, burglaries, robberies, selling false documentation, and other illicit transactions in addition to drug trafficking, not only in Madrid but also in Bilbao and southern Spain. Quick to anger and resort to violence, Jamal always carried weapons with him and very quickly developed a fearsome reputation on the street that only facilitated his dirty business activities. He also drank, popped pills, snorted drugs himself, and initially spent time partying, both with Spanish women and in Moroccan discotheques. That temporary hedonistic phase was curtailed somewhat in the summer of 1992, when he met and fell in love with a Spanish heroin addict named Rosa, whom he thenceforth doted on to the point that he helped her kick her drug habit and reconcile her with her estranged mother. During a visit home in 1993, he stabbed a lad who was trying to steal from him while he was asleep in a taxi, but fled back to Spain before he could be prosecuted.[148]

How did this troubled criminal end up embracing Islamism and being associated with the jihadist cell that carried out the Madrid bombings? Some have suggested that, after being arrested for trafficking in December 1993 and then sentenced to 2 years in the Carabanchel and Valdemoro prisons, where he became temporarily addicted to heroin, he first sought solace in Islam in an effort to end his drug dependency.[149] When he was released in October 1995, he became increasingly religious, stopped taking drugs, and pressured other Arabs near the local garage mosque not to get high.[150] Moreover, he started spending time discussing Islam with the imam at that same mosque, as well as paying a portion of the proceeds from his illicit activities in the form of alms (*zakat*) to the M-30 and Abu Bakr mosques in Madrid.[151] However, it seems to have been his growing anger and ever-increasing sense of victimization after successive arrests that really led to his radicalization. In 1998, he emerged from a stint in a French prison with a beard and a temporary desire to pray five times per day, and began obsessing about the plight of the Chechens and Palestinians.[152] On a 1999 business trip to Amsterdam, he was further radicalized by the imam of a small mosque, to which he then made a charitable contribution.[153] In March 2001 he was arrested with false documents and imprisoned again, this time in the Centro de Inmigrantes Extranjeros (Center for Foreign Immigrants[CIE]) in Madrid, which prompted him to become the de facto leader of the other prisoners and to adopt an increasingly hostile attitude towards his "infidel" country of residence.[154] He actually managed to escape from the CIE on April 16, 2000, at which point he went out of his way to call his former guards to threaten and taunt them. In December 2000 he returned to Morocco to straighten out his identity documentation problems, but was arrested there within a few days for the murder of the boy he had stabbed years before.[155] He spent over 3 years in a Moroccan prison, during which time — like many other Muslim petty criminals who have gone through similar experiences — he completed his radicalization process and began nursing a desire to kill the enemies of Allah. He was also apparently angered by the U.S. invasion of Iraq.

Hence by the time he was released from prison in the summer of 2003, Ahmidan was ideologically and psychologically primed to join a jihadist cell, and his fortuitous encounter with Fakhit later that year soon led to his active involvement in the 3/11 plot. Moreover, despite his frequently reckless behavior, even in the weeks before the attacks,[156] he was a great asset to the cell because he possessed good organizational skills, had considerable experience conducting clandestine activities, and had the sort of personal charisma that made him a good leader who could inspire others.

It again needs to be emphasized that the first two of the three above figures, all of whom played important roles in the 3/11 cell, had been affiliated for years with jihadist networks in Spain and beyond. As a result, they were heavily influenced by and often interacted personally with a host of veteran jihadists, including those who were associated with al-Qa'ida, the GICM, and other terrorist groups. Indeed, these webs of interconnections, both among cell members and between them and other jihadists, were so dense and extensive that the 2004 Spanish indictment against the surviving plotters devoted over 500 pages to tracing the cell members' phone contacts and interactions (since many of their phone calls were by then being monitored and recorded by the police).[157] The indictment then spent another 100 pages tracing their contacts with jihadists in Belgium, France, Italy, and Morocco, including details about the post-attack flights of al-Falah and al-Hajj, on the basis of information found in judicial investigations carried out in those countries.[158] It is precisely because of their extensive contacts and frequent interactions with jihadist operatives linked to al-Qa'ida, the GICM or al-Salafiyya al-Jihadiyya, and the GIA that many observers have concluded, rightly or wrongly, that the attacks were secretly sponsored, guided, or directed by higher-ups within those veteran organizations.[159] Since the general impact of al-Qa'ida operatives on the recruitment and radicalization of certain cell members has been discussed above, and the cell's main link to the GIA was through al-Amari, about whose importance there is considerable debate, a bit more information should be provided on the cell's Moroccan connections.

In this context, the key figures involved are al-Maymuni, al-'Azizi, al-Hajj, and Hasan al-Haski. As has been noted, the role of al-Maymuni was central to the development of the 3/11 cell since he was the leader of the Spanish al-Salafiyya al-Jihadiyya group, one of the two intersecting groups from which that cell emerged. Had he not gone to Morocco to organize new jihadist cells and plan attacks there, perhaps including the 2003 Casablanca suicide bombings, he may well have ended up as an integral member of the Madrid operational cell. Like Abu Dahdah, al-Maymuni had earlier helped recruit volunteers to wage jihad in Afghanistan and Chechnya, and according to his close comrade al-'Azizi, after Abu Dahdah's arrest he formed two cells that were integrated into al-Qa'ida, one in Spain (presumably the al-Salafiyya al-Jihadiyya group) and one in the Moroccan town of Kanitra, which was later implicated in the 2003 Casablanca attacks.[160]

As for al-'Azizi, he was a veteran *mujahid* who had received training in terrorist camps, first in the Bosnian industrial town of Zenica and then later in Afghanistan.[161] Indeed, according to some accounts, he served as Abu Mus'ab al-Suri's protégé at the al-Ghuraba' camp in Afghanistan, or as an instructor (together with al-Suri) in the Abu Khabab camp in the Darunta complex.[162] Whatever the specifics, he was regarded as a "big fish" who had direct connections with al-Qa'ida Central and later became Abu Dahdah's right-hand man in Spain.[163] He has also been portrayed as "the leader of the GICM," which many regard as Morocco's primary al-Qa'ida affiliate.[164] Some have further claimed that he provided organizational and logistical assistance to the 9/11 plotters during their summer 2001 meetings in northeastern Spain—of interest in this context is that his phone number was found in the phone book of Zakariyyas Musawi, a projected participant in "second wave" al-Qa'ida attacks inside the United States in the wake of "blessed Tuesday"— and he subsequently exerted a strong influence over the group headed by al-Maymuni after Abu Dahdah's arrest.[165] Moreover, he was a key participant at an important February 2002 jihadist summit in Istanbul, where the representatives of numerous North African terrorist groups, including several that were affiliated with al-Qa'ida, gathered to devise a new strategy in response to the American overthrow of the Taliban regime. At that meeting, a decision was reportedly made to launch new waves of terrorist attacks, including inside Western countries. Some have argued that plans to attack Spain, which later materialized on 3/11, were hatched at that meeting.[166]

Yusuf bin al-Hajj was yet another member of the GICM with close links to al-Qa'ida who was later suspected of being the mastermind of the 3/11 bombings. He set up a base of operations in Belgium, and regularly used a network he had established there to repatriate Afghan veterans to their countries of origin or find them refuge elsewhere, as well as to help fugitive terrorists escape from European police dragnets.[167] Among other things, he helped facilitate the post-3/11 flight from Spain of both his own brother Muhammad (who had been in the apartment at Leganés but had left before the police cordoned it off and laid siege to it) and al-Falah, and also the latter's subsequent transit to Iraq.[168] In 2001, Yusuf had held several meetings in a mosque in Leganés with al-Falah, his brother Maymun, his nephews the Musatin brothers, and Abu Shar to discuss jihad and going to fight in Afghanistan. However, the oddest fact in the accusations leveled against al-Hajj is that on October 19, 2003, 1 day after al-Jazira broadcast a public statement by Usama bin Ladin threatening Spain for its involvement in Iraq, he bought a new Belgian mobile phone, for which he provided a false name and the incorrect birth date of March 11, 1921, information that was then entered into the phone's SIM card. Not only did al-Hajj know that this particular month and day fell shortly before the following year's Spanish elections, but he also apparently believed that it was exactly 2 1/2 years after the 9/11 attacks. One might assume that it was a sheer coincidence that the month and day happened to correspond to those of the future 3/11 attacks had not al-Hajj provided another false date of birth that was entered into the SIM card of his other cell phone — May 16, 1985 — the month and day of which happened to correspond, also in advance, to those of the Casablanca bombings in 2003.[169] Whether he intentionally selected those dates in order to secretly alert his contacts in Madrid, including cell member Abu Shar, about exactly when their projected attacks were to be launched, as the public prosecutor claimed, is unclear.

A final GICM operative who was accused at one point of being the "planner" of the Madrid bombings was Hasan al-Haski. Between 2000 and 2002, al-Haski lived in the Canary Islands in Las Palmas, but at the end of 2002 he went to Syria, ostensibly to deepen his knowledge of Islamic theology.[170] However, in his capacity as a GICM leader, he spent much of his time there indoctrinating a group of Syrians, Algerians, and Moroccans whom he was preparing to send to Iraq via Turkey. While in Syria he also met with Muhsin Khaybar, who was later implicated in the 2003 Casablanca bombings, to discuss the future leadership of the GICM, and later attended a meeting in the Belgian town of Genk, at which 'Abd al-Qadir Hakimi and other representatives of the organization allegedly devised a common strategy and discussed who would succeed its current *'amir*. In February and early March of 2004 al-Haski stayed with various "brothers" in France, but appeared to be very nervous and restless, perhaps because he knew about the forthcoming attacks. After 3/11 he suddenly became calm, claimed that the train bombings had been carried out by *his* "group" (*jama'a*), and openly expressed both pride and satisfaction about the successful results of the operation. Nonetheless, between mid-April and early May, he traveled back to the Canaries.[171]

Given that so many GICM operational leaders were linked, at various points, to members of the 3/11 cell, it is no wonder that both the GICM itself and the transnational network it had affiliated itself with, that of al-Qa'ida, were both depicted as the sponsors or masterminds of the Madrid bombings. Nor were such charges leveled solely against Moroccan extremists. The same was also true of Rabi' 'Uthman al-Sayyid Ahmad (Muhammad the Egyptian), a key figure in al-Qa'ida's logistical network in Italy who had extensive interactions with the "brothers" in the Abu Dahdah network, its reconfigured successors, and the 3/11 cell itself, right up until a few weeks before the attacks. His long-standing role in radicalizing, recruiting, and then transferring European militants to jihadist fronts elsewhere has been thoroughly documented in the course of a series of Italian judicial investigations and trials. He was born in Egypt in 1971, had a degree in electronics from an Egyptian technical school, and served in the Egyptian army—specifically the specialized Explosives Brigade in Port Said—for 5 years. However, he was also secretly a member of the Tanzim al-Jihad al-Islami, and was therefore imprisoned during the mid-1990s in Abu Zaba'al jail.[172] He later made his way to Europe, and was arrested in Germany in 1999 after trying to cross the border into France without proper papers. He then falsely claimed to be a Palestinian refugee and was sent to a camp in Lebech for asylum seekers whose applications were being processed, where he became the principal imam, a position he used to spread radical Islamist doctrines. He managed to escape from the lightly guarded camp, and then made his way, first to Spain in January 2001 to find a wife, then to France to make contact with jihadist circles, then back to Spain to continue radicalizing and recruiting jihadists, and still later to Italy to establish a new base of operations.[173]

Following the arrest of his collaborator Abu Dahdah, Muhammad the Egyptian assumed a much greater leadership role in Spanish jihadist circles after gathering some of the former's men together and forming a new group in Lavapiés, one that included several of the later 3/11 cell members, including Ghalyun and Amghar. Members of his group also increasingly interacted with the "brothers" in the above-mentioned group led by al-Maymuni, which included Fakhit. Indeed, Ahmad and al-Maymuni had both spent considerable time recruiting and radicalizing militants at the M-30 mosque.[174] Although Ahmad left Spain at the very end of January 2004, only a few weeks before the train attacks, a witness claimed that he had previously seen him at the Chinchón house.[175] This in turn caused some analysts to speculate that Ahmad was not only a key planner behind the bombings, but also that he may have provided instructions on how to fabricate bombs directly to certain 3/11 cell members.[176] Several phone calls that were subsequently intercepted by the Italian police seemed to support the interpretation that Ahmad was involved in planning the action. For example, in a May 24, 2004, conversation with a would-be Moroccan "martyr" living in Belgium named Murad al-Shabaru (whom he had known since they first met in Tarazona in 2002), Ahmad made an allusion to the Madrid bombers and referred to them as "the boys," "our friends," "my brother" Sirhan [Fakhit], and the rest of "the brothers," all of whom "went to Allah."[177] Two days later, in a conversation with a young Palestinian protégé named Yahya Bayuni, who Ahmad was grooming to be a martyr, the latter said:

> There is one thing that I am not going to hide from you: [lowering his voice] the attack in Madrid was my project and those who died [as] martyrs are my very dear friends. . . . I am the thread of Madrid, when the deed happened I wasn't there, but I'll tell you the truth, before the operation, on the 4th, I had contacts with them . . . keep your mouth shut . . . I go around alone, [but] they worked in [a] group. . . . Five [sic] died martyrs and eight have been arrested; they are the best friends, dearest friends, very loyal . . . already on the 4th I began to plan, but at a high level, I wanted to plan it so that it was something that was unforgettable. . . . I wanted a big load but I couldn't find the means. The plan cost me a lot of money and patience, it took me 2 1/2 years . . . beware!! . . . Don't you ever mention anything. . . .[178]

Even if one assumes that Ahmad was simply a blabbermouth and a braggart who exaggerated his own role rather than one of the actual planners of the attack or instead concludes, as the Spanish judges did, that the translation of this last conversation was flawed and that he had really said something else,[179] there can no doubt whatsoever that members of the group he led in Spain, along with members of the group headed by al-Maymuni, later went on to join forces and carry out the 3/11 attacks. Hence at the very least, Ahmad played a significant role in helping to reorganize elements of Abu Dahdah's recently decapitated al-Qa'ida network in Spain into a new cell, as well as in instigating, directly or indirectly, the attacks that followed by incessantly urging his followers to wage jihad.

Be that as it may, the identification by investigators, both official and unofficial, of a seemingly endless succession of alleged "intellectual authors" of the Madrid bombings has given free rein to cynical or conspiratorially-minded critics of the constantly shifting official version. For example, De Pablo has sardonically noted that the prosecutors and judges had identified no less than 10 individuals as the "masterminds" of the attacks, but that none of them were actually charged (and many were not even mentioned) in either the 2007 sentence or that of the Appeals Court 1 year later.[180] However, the failure to definitively identify such a person or group, at least thus far, does not necessarily mean that there were no intellectual authors behind the material perpetrators. Indeed, such intellectual authors must have existed, even if they were to be found among the material perpetrators rather than hypothesized secret sponsors or behind-the-scenes controllers.

Unfortunately, the problems involved in tracing the ultimate sponsors or masterminds of the 3/11 attacks—if indeed they exist—are formidable and therefore difficult to resolve, simply because of the complex and fluid nature of the web of linkages and interconnections between different networks, organizations, and cells that make up the global jihadist milieu. Perhaps the best summary of these problems, in reference to the relationships between al-Qa'ida, the GICM, and local cells, has been provided by Malika Zeghal:

> The logic that nowadays governs the constitution and evolution of jihadist terrorism is that of looser and looser networks. They are made up, on the one hand, of branches that are not necessarily structured, and about which one knows little concerning their extension, and are formed by means of individual movements and unexpected encounters in an era of [extensive] migratory movements throughout the world; and, on the other hand, of 'nodes' emerging from these encounters, which are so many cells organized in a flexible manner. These can either follow external orders or become independent; and they can easily mutate and multiply independently of any command center, such as that of al-Qaida, while still remaining inspired by it.[181]

This concise but shrewd characterization accurately describes the ongoing organizational shift away from the sort of hierarchically-structured terrorist groups that constituted the norm in the late 1960s and 1970s towards more decentralized, diffuse, and loose network structures.

The decentralized and compartmentalized GICM network shares those very same traits, since its nodes are effectively led by different 'umara operating in the field rather than by its nominal supreme leaders. As one Spanish journalist described the situation:

It is extremely difficult, not only to determine the configuration of the operational leadership of the GICM, but also to identify its structure, its degree of national implantation, and its international connections, of which tentacles have been detected in Spain, Great Britain, Belgium, Italy, Turkey, and Denmark. It is a design with a special role [*protagonismo*] for insulated cells and independent elements with a scant or non-existent level of knowledge concerning the "grand strategy" of [the parent] organization, which recruits operatives who have been tied to Salafism, both in Morocco and in the Muslim community implanted in Europe.[182]

Moreover, the GICM, which was initially formed (as the Harakat al-Islamiyya al-Maghribiyya [Moroccan Islamic Movement]) in Peshawar in 1993 by Moroccan veterans of the Afghan war, trained Moroccan operatives in the Abu Khabab camp, and endeavored to forge a common North African jihadist front with the GIA, GSPC, and the Tanzim al-Jihad, was reconstituted in 1998, in part to facilitate the execution of attacks encouraged or sponsored by al-Qa'ida Central within its own geographic spheres of operation. The GICM's cells in North Africa and Europe were not part of the organic structure of al-Qa'ida, but could nonetheless act in support of that organization's broader objectives or aid al-Qa'ida operatives logistically.[183] Hence, according to Merlos, Spanish Socialist Workers Party (Partido Socialista Obrore Espanol [PSOE]) leader José Luis Rodríguez Zapateros oversimplified greatly when he claimed that the 9/11 and 3/11 attacks were completely different in terms of their motivational, organizational, and operational matrix. On the contrary, all of the different levels of jihadist networks intermingled in complex ways in the period leading up to the 3/11 attacks.[184] This does not mean, however, that one can trace a clear line of authorship behind those attacks leading from al-Qa'ida Central to the leaders of the GICM to the members of the Madrid cell, since we are dealing with a decentralized al-Qa'ida network, a decentralized GICM network, and individual cells that were linked to elements of both in a very convoluted and confusing fashion.

However that may be, Zeghal's above-cited description does not quite conform to John Arquilla's interesting notions about "all-channel" or "swarming" networks, much less to other theories postulating the primacy of "leaderless resistance" or autonomous "self-generating" cells with no meaningful links to other organizations and networks.[185] This is because in the real world, various jihadist cells or groupuscules (i.e., "grouplets") that suddenly coalesce — whether in accordance with pre-established plans or spontaneously and unexpectedly — may in some instances end up following orders issued by other, more influential and resource-rich organizations or networks to which they have become affiliated, on other occasions decide to collaborate on an ad hoc basis with other cells in order to facilitate the carrying out of particular actions, and at still other times be acting entirely on their own initiative. Indeed, the very same grouplet may well shift back and forth between these distinct and seemingly antithetical behavioral patterns. Since those three patterns are not necessarily mutually exclusive, either in time or in space, the resulting organizational and interactive fluidity makes it all the more difficult for outsiders to determine exactly when particular cells may be acting independently and when they may be cooperating with or acting at the behest of other parties. This is certainly the case with the Madrid bombings.

For that very reason, it is possible to view the 3/11 plot as either the product of schemes hatched by elements from veteran foreign terrorist organizations with which several cell members had been or still were linked, including al-Qa'ida and the GICM, or to view it as an action that was undertaken more or less independently and on the personal initiative of key figures within that cell. Thus, there is a fairly wide spectrum of reasonable interpretations that could conceivably be derived from the existing facts, but the truth surely lies between the two opposite poles on that interpretive spectrum. Indeed, *the two interpretations that are the least likely to be true* are those at the termini of this wide spectrum of possibilities: 1) that the *majlis al-shura* of al-Qa'ida (i.e., al-Qa'ida Central) directly ordered the attacks, or 2) that they were carried out independently by a "self-starter" cell without assistance of any kind from jihadists in other organizations. Unfortunately, this latter view has currently become the accepted wisdom, in part because it has been reinforced by the excessive caution of certain trial and appellate judges, who ended up concluding that the 3/11 attacks were not only "without intellectual authorship," an absurd claim, but also that there was no meaningful involvement at all by personnel from other jihadist cells or networks. While the more extravagant claims attributing sponsorship or planning of the bombings to the leadership directorates of al-Qa'ida or the GICM remain unconvincing, since the evidence cited in support of those claims is at best only suggestive, it is also difficult if not impossible to accept the seemingly naïve verdicts rendered by the two courts, which in the end concluded that there was no form of external involvement in the 3/11 operation—despite the wealth of documented connections between cell members and other jihadist circles, both in the recent past and even, in some cases, in the days leading up to the attacks.

In this context, it should be emphasized that judicial decisions should never be regarded as infallible or as "the gospel truth." After all, judges frequently make errors in judgment and other types of mistakes, like professionals in all other fields, and at times they resort to legal reasoning that is not only tortuous but also seems bizarre or even perverse.[186] Moreover, their ability to remain disinterested or objective has often been undermined by a host of other factors, such as highly politicized judiciaries (especially in countries with proportional representation) in which ideological biases of varying sorts are often blatant,[187] political pressures exerted overtly or covertly by the executive branch,[188] the corrosive impact of unofficial patronage systems marked by behind-the-scenes exchanges of reciprocal favors, flaws, or loopholes built into the structures of their nation's legal institutions,[189] and even feelings of collective societal guilt in countries with formerly dictatorial regimes (like Germany, Italy, and Spain) that abused their power egregiously and thereby destroyed the rule of law. Under such circumstances, it has all too often been the case that courts in Europe have failed to convict suspected jihadist terrorists, despite the existence of considerable amounts of evidence that pointed to their guilt, usually on the basis of seemingly spurious reasoning or by throwing out cases on the basis of technicalities.[190]

In any event, having briefly surveyed the innumerable interconnections between members of the 3/11 cell and jihadists associated with other organizations and networks, it should already be apparent that the notion that the Madrid cell was an essentially autonomous, "self-generating" cell composed of amateurish jihadist "newbies" is utterly absurd. Nor can one claim, as Atran has, that this particular cell had no significant connections, operational or otherwise, to elements of al-Qa'ida or other jihadist terrorist organizations. On the contrary, it was made up of numerous veteran militants, including several who were associated with Abu Dahdah's al-Qa'ida network in Spain. Yet Atran and others, including certain judges associated with the case, have sarcastically asked where al-Qa'ida was in the context of 3/11. This seems to be a case of ideo-logically- or conceptually-driven perceptual blind-ness, willful or otherwise, since the influence of ele-ments of al-Qa'ida and other jihadist Salafist groups was present, in a multitude of ways, during the entire historical evolution of the cell. Several points need to be emphasized in this regard.

First, it is ridiculous to argue that, unless a particu-lar cell is receiving its marching orders or extensive financial subsidies directly from Bin Ladin, al-Zawa-hiri, or other high-level figures from al-Qa'ida Cen-tral, it has no links to al-Qa'ida at all other than those of an inspirational albeit vague ideological nature. To make such an argument is fundamentally to misun-derstand the role of al-Qa'ida Central, including its operational role, in relation to that of its affiliates and local cells. In fact, even in cases where al-Qa'ida sent its own "hit teams" or intentionally implanted agents from overseas to form cells, recruit locals, and thence organize attacks in the West, it usually did not exer-cise close supervision or direct command, control, and coordination over the activities of its operatives in far-flung theatres. Far from endeavoring to mi-cromanage the activities of its operatives, even those who were carrying out strategic strikes that it had ex-plicitly authorized and partially planned, it typically left many of the actual tactical or operational details to them. This was even partly true of the spectacular 9/11 attacks, since 'Ata' was given a certain amount of leeway in planning various logistical and operational details inasmuch as he, being in the field, was in a better position to be able to adjust and adapt to new, sometimes unexpected developments that might affect the overall success of the "planes operation." In certain instances, of course, Bin Ladin insisted that his operatives abroad follow a certain pre-established plan more or less closely, but even in those cases he was not usually able to prevent them from making periodic changes or personally to exert a high degree of de facto operational control over them.

Since this has been the normal pattern, even in relation to those attacks overseas that were planned and subsidized by al-Qa'ida Central, why would anyone assume that the group's *majlis al-shura* would necessarily exercise direct operational control over the activities of local cells, including those that were linked to its affiliates, whose specific activities it did not even endeavor to guide or control? And why, for that matter, would they further assume that every cell that did not receive such close levels of central supervision, guidance, or support was entirely autonomous, unconnected, and made up of amateurish "bunches of guys"? In short, drawing a hard and fast "either/or" distinction between cells which were supposedly micromanaged by al-Qa'ida Central and those which were totally independent has unfortunately had the effect of creating a false dichotomy that rarely if ever conforms to the fluidity and complexity of the linkages within the jihadist milieu in the real world.

Second, the view of Sageman that local jihadist cells were often formed after the bottom-up recruitment

by "born again" jihadists of their friends and kinsmen — or perhaps after their top-down recruitment by
professional jihadist spotters, who found it easier to
induce such "bunches of guys" to join together — has
in my opinion been granted far too much explanatory
power. It is hardly surprising that recent Muslim immigrants living in the West, like most émigrés from
a particular region of the world who end up settling
in societies that are very different culturally, would
initially prefer to associate with their countrymen,
co-religionists, kinsmen, and friends than with alien
members of their new societies, a tendency which
almost always produces self-segregating social patterns that initially act to inhibit assimilation and ac-
culturation. To the extent that those same immigrants
are also subjected to some level of socio-economic dis-
crimination, as they often are, this will only act to further alienate them from their host societies and cause
them to associate and identify even more closely with
those with whom they share a common background.
These tendencies are arguably even more common
among Muslims, most of whom arrive in Europe from
societies that are essentially tribal in nature, where
large clans and extended families are the norm, and
where there is a pronounced, sometimes fierce loyalty
to kinsmen. Hence it should come as no surprise to
learn that when individual Muslims become so alienated that they adopt an adversarial attitude towards
their host societies and/or suffer an identity crisis that
leads them to view themselves as members of the real
or virtual *umma*, sometimes to the point of wanting to
wage jihad against the infidel societies they reside in,
that they should first approach some of their kinsmen
and friends for support and aid. Moreover, unless
they join cults whose leaders encourage them to break

their previous social ties, people are often inclined to tell their closest associates the "good news" when they have suddenly become religiously devout, and then to try to convert them to their new worldview.

This reliance on kinsmen and friends is likewise true of those individuals who had embraced an Islamist worldview even before arriving in the West, since they were already ideologically conditioned to view their new land as a part of the *dar al-harb*, i.e., as a "satanic" society filled with "infidel Crusaders" who were out to destroy Islam. For this very reason, they often eschew unnecessary contact with non-Muslims, whom they view as inherently corrupt if not thoroughly evil. At times, however, they may well seek to manipulate and make instrumental use of certain unwitting unbelievers in pursuit of their radically anti-Western objectives. It is also common for individuals who intend to engage in illicit or subversive clandestine activities to have recourse first to friends and kinsmen, which is why one so often finds close kinship relations to be characteristic of criminal gangs, organized or otherwise. It is surely no accident that criminals tend to organize themselves along ethnic lines, e.g., into the Sicilian, Corsican, Russian, Chechen, Nigerian, or Turkish mobs, the Japanese *yakuza*, the Chinese triads, etc. After all, inviting absolute strangers to join them in illegal activities would entail dangerous risks, whereas kinsmen and close friends are less likely to alert the authorities even if they opt not to participate in those types of activities. Why, then, should one find it so surprising and significant that both jihadist cells and Muslim criminal gangs in Europe are often composed largely of kinsmen and close friends from the same villages or towns in their countries of origin? In short, although Sageman is perfectly correct to point out this social fact, in the final analysis it is a rather banal observation.[191] Moreover, in and of itself this particular phenomenon is only tangentially related to the key issues involved in assessing jihadist *capabilities*, including both their overall operational effectiveness and their possession of the technical skills necessary for IED fabrication: (1) whether the members of such cells are rank amateurs or experienced veterans, and (2) whether those cells are autonomous and self-generating or are instead connected to established jihadist organizations.

What, then, are the salient facts about the members of the 3/11 operational cell? First, after Abu Dahdah's Spanish al-Qa'ida network was dismantled due to police action in November 2001, the members of that network who had escaped arrest during the sweeps either took flight or laid low until the initial crackdown had run its course. It was not long, however, before they began coalescing, reorganizing, re-establishing contact with al-Qa'ida and Moroccan jihadist operatives elsewhere in Europe, and resuming their anti-Western plotting and activities. Angered by the arrests of their "brothers" and what they perceived to be attacks on Islam at home and abroad, al-Maymuni, Fakhit, and their associates in Madrid's so-called Harakat al-Salafiyya al-Jihadiyya began meeting regularly and engaging in a series of intense debates about what actions to undertake in support of the global jihad. The key question was whether to continue recruiting and sending *mujahidin* from Europe to battlefields elsewhere (as the Abu Dahdah network had done for years), whether to go off themselves to fight on other fronts, or whether to carry out attacks in the European countries where they resided. In the end, angered by the invasion of Iraq and other international events and further inspired both by certain public exhortations of Bin Ladin and online statements by other global jihadist militants, sometime in 2003 they definitively opted to carry out attacks inside Spain itself.[192] Like many other countries in Europe, Spain was therefore transformed from a jihadist logistical "rearguard" base into a jihadist "frontline" objective or target of attack.[193] In short, what occurred was essentially a restructuring of previously existing jihadist networks, including the one that had originally been formed by al-Qa'ida operatives, not—as Atran and Sageman keep insisting—the "self-generation" of an entirely new organization by "bunches of guys" with no tangible connections to veteran past or present jihadist networks.

It should also be pointed out, parenthetically, that not even Ahmidan's criminal gang, or components thereof, could be fairly described in 2003 as a self-generating organization, since Ahmidan had initially formed his network of Moroccan criminals almost a decade earlier and still continued to direct it, even though the scale of its activities and its precise membership fluctuated over time, due in large part to periodic police crackdowns that resulted in the arrests of Ahmidan or his men. Even if that network could justly have been characterized as a self-generating criminal group way back in the mid-1990s, when it was first established, all "the Chinaman" had to do was reconstitute it when he was released from a Moroccan prison in 2003. Apart from Ahmidan's imposition of new, religiously-derived strictures on his thugs, the main change was that, in the months leading up to the bombings, some of the most trustworthy members of his crew were made aware of the projected jihadist attacks and thus became bona fide members of the 3/11 logistical cell, whereas others remained mere grunts who performed ancillary tasks but were unaware of Ahmidan's true purposes.

Second, many observers have argued that if Fakhit and his group had not befriended and collaborated with Jamal Ahmidan and his criminal gang, they would never have had the wherewithal to carry out a major terrorist attack in Spain.[194] It is of course a historical fact that the increasing interaction between Fakhit and Ahmidan did in fact initiate a sequence of events that ultimately resulted in the 3/11 train bombings, but that is no reason to draw the conclusion that Fakhit's group would have otherwise never been able to carry out such an attack. It is true that the operational group was temporarily short of resources, so much so that both Fakhit and Ahmidan made efforts to collect past debts in the weeks before 3/11,[195] but this was mainly due to the crackdown on and resulting disruption of the al-Qa'ida network and other jihadist groups in Europe in the wake of 9/11. At that particular juncture, it was indeed fortuitous that Fakhit befriended Ahmidan, and that one of Ahmidan's men put the cell members in touch with Zuhayr, who then functioned as their intermediary with the Spanish criminals selling explosives in Asturias. However, when clever extremists really have the will, they usually manage to find a way to actualize their plans, however ineptly — especially if they have had prior operational experience or receive direct guidance from others who are more operationally and technically proficient. No one can accurately predict the future course of events in an alternate history scenario that never unfolded, but *the notion that Ahmidan and his crew were the only people in Spain or Europe who could have arranged for Fakhit's acquisition of explosives is clearly unwarranted.* Indeed, given the extensive contacts that various cell members continued to maintain with other jihadists, it is entirely possible that they would have been able to exploit those contacts to find another supplier of explosives even if Ahmidan had never entered the picture. Whether obtaining dynamite and detonators from another source would have resulted in an IED attack on the Spanish railway system similar to that on 3/11 is, of course, anyone's guess.

Lastly, it is necessary to return to the categorization scheme devised and outlined above, which highlighted the fact that there are many possible levels of interaction between local cells and networks linked to al-Qa'ida or other jihadist groups, and then endeavor to place the 3/11 cell within that framework. It seems clear that the Madrid bombers straddled two of the main categories listed in the scheme first delineated above. Many of the members of that cell had, in fact, originally been indoctrinated and recruited by operatives implanted in Europe by al-Qa'ida or affiliated networks, above all the GICM. Even so, the cell does not fall unambiguously into the second category, since it may not have received ongoing assistance, however sporadic, from those parent organizations. However, it does not fall neatly into the third category either, i.e., a self-generating cell connected directly or indirectly to members of foreign jihadist networks, precisely because it was actually *formed by several individuals who had previously been recruited by or otherwise associated with cells that had been implanted by foreign organizations*. Hence, in order to fit the 3/11 case snugly into the above scheme, a new primary category needs to be added to it: jihadist cells formed by individuals who were previously recruited by and/or collaborating closely with operatives of foreign jihadist organizations. The revised scheme, with a new third category, is as follows:

1. Jihadist "hit teams" sent from abroad.

    a. jihadist "hit teams" sent to Europe from elsewhere by al-Qa'ida Central, usually after having been provided with specialized instruction (perhaps including in bomb-making skills) in training camps abroad, in order to launch terrorist operations and attacks themselves;

    b. jihadist "hit teams" sent to Europe from elsewhere by al-Qa'ida's nominal or de facto regional affiliates, perhaps after obtaining specialized training in their respective countries, in order to carry out terrorist operations and attacks themselves;

    c. jihadist "hit teams" sent to Europe from elsewhere by other veteran jihadist organizations, perhaps after obtaining specialized training in their respective countries, in order to carry out terrorist operations and attacks themselves;

2. "Local" jihadist cells organized, supported, and/or directed from abroad.

    a. "local" jihadist cells recruited and trained by al-Qa'ida operatives implanted in Europe for that very purpose, and thereafter receiving periodic assistance of various types from al-Qa'ida Central or its regional affiliates;

    b. "local" jihadist cells recruited and trained by operatives sent by other veteran jihadist groups who were implanted in Europe, sometimes for that very purpose, and thereafter receiving periodic assistance of various types from their parent organizations;

3. Local jihadist cells formed by militants who had previously been radicalized and recruited by, or otherwise closely associated with, earlier local cells established by operatives working for foreign terrorist groups.

    a. local jihadist cells formed by militants who were previously members of earlier local cells established by operatives working for al-Qa'ida Central;

    b. local jihadist cells formed by militants who were previously members of earlier local cells established by operatives working for al-Qa'ida's regional affiliates;

    c. local jihadist cells formed by militants who were previously members of earlier local cells established by operatives working for other veteran jihadist groups;

4. Connected "self-generating" European jihadist cells.

    a. "self-generating" European jihadist cells that are in *direct* contact with operatives from al-Qa'ida Central;

    b. "self-generating" European jihadist cells that are in *direct* contact with operatives from al-Qa'ida's regional affiliates;

    c. "self-generating" European jihadist cells that are in *direct* contact with operatives from other veteran jihadist groups;

    d. "self-generating" European jihadist cells that are connected *indirectly*, via intermediaries, to operatives from al-Qa'ida Central, its regional affiliates, or other veteran jihadist groups;

    e. "self-generating" European jihadist cells that are in *direct* contact with operatives from other European "self-generating" cells;

f. "self-generating" European jihadist cells that are connected *indirectly*, via intermediaries, to operatives from other European "self-generating" cells;

g. "self-generating" European jihadist cells that include individuals who are members of al-Qa'ida or other foreign terrorist networks;

5. *Isolated or fully autonomous "self-generating" European jihadist cells* that are not connected in any way to members of any other jihadist groups or cells.

Hence, the 3/11 cell best conforms to category 3, the new intermediate category that has now been added to this scheme. *Under no circumstances does it fit into category 5*, as some have suggested.

The 3/11 Cell and Bomb-Making Expertise.

In the context of IED capabilities, the one question that might be even more important than the issue of whether the Madrid terrorist cell was linked to other jihadist organizations, from which they might have obtained expert assistance directly or indirectly, is whether any individual cell members had previously acquired hands-on personal experience or expertise in manufacturing explosive devices. Unfortunately, despite the voluminous information available in the judicial materials relating to the Madrid bombings, including the exhaustive forensic detail provided in the indictments and sentences about the bombs themselves and the remains and materials found in various locales used by cell members, this is not a question that can be definitively answered. Indeed, it is not even clear exactly who actually fabricated the devices that were later placed on the trains. Hence the best that one can do at the present time is to draw tentative conclusions about these crucial matters based on the incomplete information that is currently available in the public record.

The first place to begin, however, is with a brief reconstruction of the process by which the cell members managed to acquire the explosives and detonators that were used in the 3/11 attacks. The main point that needs to be made is that virtually all of the Goma-2 ECO dynamite used in the train attacks and later detonated in the apartment in Leganés was obtained from the Conchita Mine in Asturias, which was owned by the Caolines de Merillés Company and situated in Calabazos near the Soto de la Barca dam.[196] The course of events that resulted in the use of these materials in terrorist attacks began in September 2001, when Rafa Zuhayr and Antonio Toro Castro, two petty criminals imprisoned in the Centro Penitenciaro in Villabona (Asturias), befriended each other. After being released from prison, Toro introduced Zuhayr to his brother-in-law, José Emilio Suárez Trashorras. Unbeknownst to Toro, Zuhayr had been recruited as a confidential informant by the UCO of the GC in November 2001, prior to his release, and his UCO controller was the aforementioned Víctor. In exchange for a lighter sentence, Zuhayr had agreed to provide information on various illicit criminal activities to the GC. Initially he fingered some low-level dealers, who were then investigated and arrested by the police. In February 2003, however, he told Víctor that Toro intended to sell 150 kilograms of explosives, which had been supplied to him by Suárez Trashorras, a former mineworker at the Conchita site. After tracing and locating the two men, the GC asked Zuhayr to tell the two Spaniards that he had possible buyers in Madrid, and to obtain a jar from them with some plastic explosives, which the Moroccan then delivered to GC officers at a commercial center in Madrid's Las Rozas district. Later that year, however, when he was asked to broker a deal for those explosives, Zuhayr did not inform his UCO handler because he saw it as an opportunity to make a good profit.[197]

Meanwhile, in the autumn of 2003 Jamal Ahmidan asked some of his trusted associates to find someone who could obtain explosives, although he did not tell them that a jihadist cell he was involved with needed them to carry out bomb attacks. Rashid Aklif (nicknamed "El Conejo," i.e., "the Rabbit," due to his pronounced front teeth) remembered Rafa Zuhayr, a well-connected former associate of his with whom he had collaborated on previous drug deals.[198] When Akhlif told Zuhayr that he needed explosives, Zuhayr offered to put him in contact with some criminals he knew in Asturias who trafficked in explosives and other illicit materials. After Zuhayr informed Toro that he had an interested customer, Toro and Suárez Trashorras drove to Madrid in early October and provided Zuhayr with a detonator, which the latter then displayed to Akhlif and Ahmidan at a meeting in his home on October 5, a meeting during which he accidentally triggered the detonator by applying a live wire to it, thereby slightly injuring everyone present. Three weeks later, on October 28, a meeting was arranged at a McDonald's restaurant in Madrid's Carabanchel district to finalize the deal. At that locale, Zuhayr brought Akhlif, Ahmidan, and an unidentified person to meet with Suárez Trashorras, Carmen Toro, and their friend Pablo Álvarez Moya; at the meeting Akhlif offered to make an exchange, whether of money or drugs, for 60 kilograms of dynamite. On November

17, a second meeting occurred, this time between Antonio Toro, Carmen Toro, Suárez Trashorras, Ahmidan, Zuhayr, and Akhlif at another McDonald's in the Moncloa district. Although the participants all subsequently claimed that they only spoke of drug deals at these meetings, this is scarcely believable given their frequent subsequent phone interactions and the fact that in just over a month, some of the Asturians' "couriers" began bringing explosives to Madrid.[199]

In fact, in January and early February of 2004, three shipments of explosives were transported from Asturias to Madrid.[200] On January 4, Suárez Trashorras asked one of his subordinates, Sergio Álvarez Sánchez (nicknamed "Amocachi"), to deliver a 40-kilogram bag the next day to someone who would be waiting at the Madrid bus station for it. In the mid-afternoon of January 5, Amocachi transferred the bag to Ahmidan and then boarded a bus to return to Oviedo, where he was paid in 700 euros' worth of hashish. Four days later, Suárez Trahorras sent another of his underlings, Antonio Iván Reis Palicio (nicknamed "Jimmy"), to deliver a bag of hashish to a "Moor" in Madrid, in exchange for which he would cancel an existing 3,000 euro drug debt. In this case, however, Ahmidan became annoyed with Jimmy during the exchange process, threatened to punch him, and took his mobile phone and the briefcase from him. Jimmy then returned to Oviedo empty-handed and, fearing retaliation despite Suárez Trashorras' reassurances, took off for the Canary Islands. After further interchanges with Ahmidan and the refusal of another underling named Iván Granados Peña (nicknamed "Piranha") to transport dynamite, on February 6 Suárez Trahorras sent Gabriel Montoya Vidal (nicknamed "El Gitanillo," i.e., the "Little Gypsy") to Madrid to deliver a bag full of explosives (in exchange for 1,000 euros). After arriving at the bus station, Montoya went to the Bar Virrey and called Ahmidan, using a prearranged code phrase, after which the latter arrived in a dark Opel Astra and took the bag. These and the larger quantities of explosives later sold to Ahmidan were pilfered from the Conchita mine with the connivance of certain employees there, including a security guard named Emilio Llano Álvarez, who helped "cook the books" to cover the missing explosives, and others who accepted bribes for allowing them into the mine and letting them steal various items.

Suárez Trashorras and Carmen Toro got married in mid-February, and thence went to the Canaries for their honeymoon (even though the groom continued to maintain regular phone contact with Ahmidan). This vacation, however, was rudely interrupted on February 26, when the newlyweds flew precipitously back to Madrid to meet with Ahmidan, who picked them up at the airport and drove them to the Chinchón house. Apparently, Ahmidan now wanted to acquire the rest of the explosives all at once rather than continuing to receive them in small increments. After discussing various matters, which led to a trivial spat over Mecca Cola between Carmen and Ahmidan that precipitated an Islamist rant by the latter, the parties agreed to exchange 6,000 euros and 35 kilograms of hashish for 200 kilograms of Goma-2 ECO. Suárez Trashorras and his wife then flew back to Asturias.[201] Two days later, Ahmidan drove from Madrid to Asturias with Muhammad Awlad and Kunja'a. After hooking up with Suárez Trashorras in Avilés, they followed the latter and Montoya to the area of the Conchita mine. Ahmidan and Suárez Trashorras then walked along a dangerous, icy path until they reached a certain loca-

104

tion near the mine, after which they came back and the three Moroccans drove to the nearby Carrefour commercial center, where they bought backpacks, sports bags, flashlights, gloves, batteries, food, and other items. The trio then returned by car to that same spot followed by Montoya, who waited nearby in his freezing car, and then spent several hours going back and forth up and down the path in order to collect the stolen explosives that had been placed there, which they then stored in their vehicle. All four men then drove to Avilés, where they stored the materials in Suárez Trashorras' garage. They then returned to Conchitas and collected more explosives, after which they returned to the garage and transferred everything they had gathered into another car.[202]

The following day, instead of traveling directly from Asturias to the Chinchón house to unload his dangerous and illegal cargo, Ahmidan called al-Ghanawi and asked him to drive north towards Burgos and bring Rifa'at, Rashid Awlad, and a "large nail" (the cell's code word for a rifle) with him. Ahmidan and his two companions then drove, in very treacherous winter conditions, in a caravan of two cars towards Burgos. On the way, in Sotopalacios, Ahmidan was recorded driving too fast and was pulled over by GC officers who—astonishingly given that the car was stolen and had false registration, that Ahmidan had a forged Belgian passport, and that knives and other incriminating materials were found in the car—simply issued fines for three minor offenses and let him go on his way. The three cars full of Ahmidan's men then rendezvoused in Burgos, for reasons unknown. Later that evening, they drove down from Burgos together in a three-car "caravan of death" to the Chinchón house, where they unloaded a substantial portion of the bomb materials they had collected.[203] In order to facilitate the storage and concealment of those materials, Ahmidan's brother Hamid and al-Ghanawi dug a large hole in the ground under a shed next to the house, which they lined with a synthetic expanded polystyrene (EPS) material called "porespán" and then covered it in such a way that it was indistinguishable from the soil around it.[204]

It is at this crucial point that vital details about the fabrication of the bombs become somewhat murky, in particular exactly when this process commenced and precisely who actually constructed the devices that were used on 3/11. There is no doubt, however, that the Chinchón house had been owned since 1997 by Nayat Fadl Muhammad, the wife of Muhammad Nidal, a Syrian who was arrested along with Abu Dahdah and other al-Qa'ida cell members in November 2001, or that it had thence been rented by Nidal's brother Walid al-Taraki to the Moroccan jihadist al-Maymuni in 2002. After he moved out, the property was listed for rent by the Arconsa company (owned by the Rustam brothers from Syria), where Fakhit worked selling real estate.[205] Apparently, Ahmidan himself began hanging out at the property as early as November 2003, although he did not officially rent it (under the pseudonym Yusuf ibn Salah) until January 2004. At some point he also began holding weekend get-togethers there with his friends and co-conspirators, including Fakhit, Zugham, the Awlad brothers, Amghar, and 'Abd al-Rahim al-Zabak (nicknamed "El Químico," i.e., "the Chemist"), another Moroccan from Tangiers who had an academic background in the chemical sciences.[206] The general consensus of the Spanish police investigators is that it was not until a week or so before the attacks that members of the cell actually began manufacturing the IEDs, and it was not until the night before that the phones were activated and the timers and detonators tested. In this connection, some have claimed that Ahmidan told many of his closest associates to stay away from the Chinchón house in the 2 weeks prior to the 3/11 attacks.[207] Nevertheless, both eyewitness testimony and forensic evidence of various kinds, including fingerprints and DNA residues, demonstrated that several associates of Ahmidan and Fakhit had spent time at that locale in recent months. Among these were Ahmidan and Fakhit themselves, Jamal's brothers Hisham and Hamid, Zugham, al-Zabak, Awnani, Abu Shar, and al-Ghanawi.[208]

However that may be, a lack of specific and verifiable information, due in part to the fact that those who might have shed light on these matters "martyred" themselves in Leganés, has made it practically impossible for outsiders to determine exactly who was entrusted with building the bombs. As a result, there has been an understandable degree of unconfirmed — and perhaps unconfirmable — speculation about who, in fact, was directly involved, whether by serving as the primary bomb maker(s) or by carrying out various peripheral tasks, which has in turn led to the promulgation of contrasting theories, conspiratorial or otherwise. For example, certain Spanish policemen operated under the assumption that unscrupulous miners who were familiar with explosives, like Suárez Trashorras, showed Ahmidan how to make bombs.[209] In contrast, two Spanish journalists have suggested that once the cell members had acquired the dynamite and detonators, all they had to do was follow the instructions found in an online al-Qa'ida manual that they had downloaded from the Internet, just as the

2003 Casablanca bombers had earlier done.[210] Other analysts, instead, have implied that certain individuals within the jihadist milieu that seem to have had the requisite levels of technical knowledge—such as Muhammad the Egyptian or Sa'ad Husayni, head of the GICM's military committee and an explosives expert—may have provided guidance if not hands-on assistance.[211] On the other hand, some observers with a more conspiratorial mindset have hypothesized that the cell members had obtained such technical assistance from professional bomb makers outside of the jihadist milieu, whether a group of *etarras* or personnel associated with various secret services.[212] Alas, as noted above, it is not presently possible to identify who actually fabricated the explosive devices used in the Madrid bombings. Hence it is also not yet possible to use the 3/11 case to test our tentative general hypothesis that, in the absence of experienced bomb makers, it is far less likely that jihadist cells will be able to carry out highly destructive IED attacks, much less longer-term IED campaigns.

Nevertheless, despite these important factual lacunae concerning the bomb-making process and the key participants in it at various stages, the Madrid case still serves to highlight many of the issues that are—and are likely to remain—vitally important for assessing the operational capabilities of jihadist cells in Western countries, including the potential IED threat that they might end up posing. This is especially true with respect to the importance of their direct and indirect connections to components of other jihadist networks, whether they are based in Muslim countries abroad or elsewhere in Europe itself. In the process, as emphasized above, it enables us to undermine, though not entirely demolish, certain problematic notions currently being peddled by Sageman and his acolytes concerning the supposedly amateurish, unconnected nature of jihadist cells in the West.

At the same time, the Madrid case also illustrates just how important blind luck and a host of other serendipitous factors might be in leading to successful or unsuccessful attacks. After all, the members of the 3/11 cell made numerous mistakes in tradecraft, ranging from engaging in reckless behavior on the eve of the attacks that could easily have resulted in the derailment of the entire plot due to leaving vital evidence, both at the scene of the attacks and elsewhere. In the final analysis, it was perhaps only the much greater blunders committed by the security forces, including repeatedly ignoring or failing to act upon vital information obtained from confidential informants or during the course of the decade-long close surveillance of many of the cell members, that made it possible for the attacks to be carried out successfully on March 11. *One point that must always be kept in mind is that "to err is human," for oftentimes the success or failure of a particular terrorist plot is primarily determined by which side makes more errors, or more serious errors, or errors at more crucial junctures.* Since in these contexts one is always dealing with intrinsically flawed human beings and not perfectly-functioning machines, predictive efforts undertaken in the counterterrorism realm must never ignore or minimize human foibles and fallibilities — either our enemies' or our own.

THE JULY 2006 GERMAN TRAIN BOMBINGS

At 11:00 am on July 31, 2006, two young Lebanese Islamists residing in Germany exited an apartment on Peter-Bauer-Strasse and took a train from the Ehrenfeld district in Cologne to the city's central train station. One of them, Yusuf Muhammad al-Hajj Dib, then boarded Train RE 12519 from Mönchengladbach to Coblenz, placed a suitcase with an IED inside in one of the cars, and then exited the train. The other, Jihad Hamad, took Train RE 10121 from Aachen to Hamm, deposited a second suitcase bomb in the car he was riding in, and exited the train at the Deutz station. Al-Hajj Dib had set the timing devices in the bombs for 2:35 p.m., at which point RE 12519 would have been in the vicinity of the Urmiz-Rhein bridge stop and RE 10121 would have been passing the Kamen station. Had the explosives detonated, 50-60 people who were in the same car in the former train would likely have been killed instantly, whereas about 15 would have been immediately killed in the latter train. However, a minor mistake made by al-Hajj Dib in the process of constructing the bombs caused both devices to fail to detonate, thereby inadvertently saving the lives — according to the German authorities — of perhaps hundreds of people. At 2:55 that same afternoon, both men left Germany on Turkish Airlines' flight TK 1672, bound for Istanbul. They then proceeded to Tripoli, where al-Hajj Dib's older brother Khalid Khayr al-Din al-Hajj Dib (alias Abu 'Abd al-Rahman) waited for them. Both terrorists planned to go on to Iraq to wage jihad against the Americans, but 7 days after the attempted bombings al-Hajj Dib's father persuaded his son Yusuf to return to Germany to complete his studies. Two weeks later, the Bundeskriminalamt (Federal Criminal [Police] Office [BKA]) released the surveillance videos from the Cologne train station, which apparently caused al-Hajj Dib to panic. Fortunately, a message sent by the BKA's liaison officer in Beirut at 8:51 that same evening to his colleagues back home revealed that a Lebanese student in Kiel was planning to leave Germany hastily and travel to Sweden to stay with his sister. A special police unit then arrested al-Hajj Dib in the Kiel central station at 3:53 a.m. After his arrest, the police searched his student residence at Steenbeker Weg 20 and found various incriminating materials.[213] His partner Hamad was then arrested in Lebanon.

It soon became clear that Yusuf al-Hajj Dib and his brother Khalid had been radicalized quite some time before, since the police found last wills and testaments on the former's computer prepared by both of them, in the latter's case dating to the end of 2005. Indeed, Khalid's home in Sweden was said to be a meeting place for Islamist extremists.[214] On the other hand, Yusuf seems to have played an instrumental role in radicalizing Hamad and involving him in this failed terrorist plot. According to the testimony of Hamad, he first became acquainted with al-Hajj Dib through his cousin, after which the duo began exchanging emails and phone calls. In April 2006 Hamad traveled from Cologne to Kiel, where al-Hajj Dib was taking a university preparatory course for foreign students, and temporarily moved in with him. Al-Hajj Dib immediately began showing the impressionable Hamad jihadist propaganda, including videos of *mujahidin* in combat, speeches by Bin Ladin broadcast on al-Jazira, *fatwa*s condemning both the U.S. invasions of Muslim countries, and the publication of the cartoons of Muhammad by a Danish newspaper (which Hamad had never seen before).[215] He then began urging him to join the struggle, insisting that his services were needed and asking if he would be willing to participate in an attack. By the late spring of 2006, Hamad himself had fully embraced al-Qa'ida's global jihadist ideology, crammed his laptop with jihadist materials, and was posting messages on a jihadist blogsite under the name "deutscherhamad" ("German Hamad"), using a picture of Abu Mus'ab al-Zarqawi to identify himself. As Hamad later put it, "Yusuf had me in his thrall."[216]

Moreover, according to Hamad, al-Hajj Dib was already trawling the Internet for instructions about how to make bombs, and by mid-May the pair had begun planning terrorist attacks in Germany. Their original plan had been to set off bombs in a packed stadium during the June-July Fédération International de Football Association (International Federation of Association Soccer [FIFA]) World Cup matches, or perhaps (if photos found in Hamad's cell phone are indicative) in Cologne's city center. In June, al-Hajj Dib showed Hamad a video in Arabic, entitled "The Use of the Gas Canister as an Explosive Charge," that he had downloaded from a jihadist website, a video that provided relative amateurs with instructions about how to use materials obtained from building supply stores to make bombs that would be cheap to manufacture and highly destructive in their effects.[217] The two then endeavored to follow those instructions by purchasing two canisters of propane gas labeled "Tyczka" from Bauhaus stores (one in Cologne and the other in Frechen), alarm clocks, and batteries in a One Euro department store in their neighborhood, and four and a half liters of gasoline and diesel fuel from a nearby Shell garage. They then used the assembled ingredients to fabricate bombs that Hamad initially admitted were designed "to kill as many people as possible."[218] Finally, al-Hajj Dib attached an alarm clock to a cable to test whether the Christmas light bulbs he had gotten would light up, which they did, thereby seemingly demonstrating that the clock could ignite the device. Tests later conducted by the Bundesanstalt für Materialforschung und-Prüfung (Federal Institute for Material Research and Testing [BAM]) revealed the devastating impact that such devices could potentially have, since if they were also filled with oxygen, they could produce a fireball with a diameter of up to 15 meters and discharge shrapnel that could reach as far as 100 meters. If diesel was added to the mixture, as al-Hajj Dib and Hamad had done, the size of the fireball could be further augmented.[219] To make matters worse, the pair had added bags of corn starch to one of the suitcase bombs so that the powder therein would be transformed by the explosion into a type of napalm that would have covered the passengers with a scorching oil film.[220] That is why the German authorities concluded that, had the two devices exploded, it could have been one of the worst Islamist terrorist attacks on European soil.

Unlike in the case of the Madrid bombings, fortunately, there are far fewer mysteries about the provenance of the information used by the German train bombers to fabricate their suitcase bombs, and there was no doubt at all that they themselves constructed the devices. However, chemists at the BKA believed that the video lacked certain vitally important information that limited its usefulness for novices unfamiliar with pressurized gases. As a result, due to the way the devices were constructed, it would have been impossible for them to detonate because the mixture of gasoline and oxygen that was needed to ignite them was absent. In short, the two would-be jihadists were unable to insert a specific oxygen mixture into the bottles (a technique shown in the video), so there was only "one fuel and one adequate ignition source," which in lieu of an oxidizing agent is not enough for a functioning bomb.[221] Indeed, according to Bodo Plewinsky, an explosives expert, "the bombs were built rather amateurishly."[222] Later, Hamad contradicted his earlier testimony by claiming that the pair had intentionally placed nonfunctioning suitcase devices in the trains as a protest against the Danish publication of the Muhammad cartoons, but this belated claim is scarcely credible, given all of the other indicators that he and al-Hajj Dib had planned to carry out a mass casualty attack.

Hence it is clear that the bomb plot initiated by the two men failed simply because they had made a crucial technical mistake that prevented the devices they had constructed from exploding. This case therefore suggests that, in the absence of requisite levels of technical proficiency, it will remain difficult for would-be jihadists to carry out successful IED attacks, which is exactly what one would expect. On the one hand, experts often find technical mistakes in the bomb-making manuals posted on the Internet, which would obviously create problems even if particular individuals followed those recommendations precisely. On the other, rank amateurs may not be able to follow the instructions in manuals to the letter, especially if they are somewhat complicated, even if the information therein turns out to be accurate. In short, if a combination of deficiencies in operational tradecraft and built-in technical limitations is likely to undermine the ability of inexperienced jihadist cell members to carry out even one highly destructive IED attack, these same obstacles would surely inhibit their prosecution of longer-term IED campaigns.

A few final remarks should be made about the apparent international connections of the two German train bombers, even though those connections might have had no direct relevance, at least in this particular instance, to their efforts to fabricate IEDs. Hamad initially claimed that their bomb attacks were motivated by anger over the publication of the Muhammad cartoons. However, it soon became clear that this was a bogus rationale, given that al-Hajj Dib and several of his relatives, even those back in Lebanon, had long embraced radical Islamist and pro-jihadist ideologies. At most, then, the cartoons simply provided one more pretext, not that any were needed given their worldview, to justify their pre-existing desire to carry out attacks on the "infidels." In actuality, as journalist Hubert Gude notes, al-Hajj Dib and Hamad can "no longer be assumed to be two simple-minded Lebanese students who had mutated into extremists in Germany on their own initiative," since "[a]ccording to Hamad, the militant duo maintained close contacts with radical warriors of God [*Gotteskriegern*], both at home and abroad."[223]

Among the groups that al-Hajj Dib may have been indoctrinated and/or influenced by, both in Lebanon and in Germany, was the Hizb al-Tahrir al-Islami (Islamic Liberation Party [HT]), which was originally founded in Jordan in the 1950s but is now headquartered in London and has branches throughout Europe and Central Asia. The ultimate agenda of this cult-like group is extremely radical and thoroughly anti-democratic and anti-Western: to re-establish the Caliphate and thence complete the Islamization of the *dar al-harb* through a combination of *da'wa* (missionary work) and armed jihad.[224] Although the organization publicly claims to be nonviolent, its actual view is that it is permissible for Muslims to wage "defensive jihad" anytime that Islam comes under attack, whereas "offensive jihad" can only be undertaken after the re-establishment of the Caliphate, since only a legitimate

Caliph can authorize it. Moreover, there is evidence that HT has frequently served as an ideological incubator for individual Muslims who thence went on to join jihadist groups, which raises the question of whether the organization functions, inadvertently or consciously, as a kind of de facto "transmission belt" for jihadist organizations. However that may be, the German authorities were sufficiently alarmed about HT's openly anti-Semitic activities that they officially banned the group on January 15, 2003.[225] Nevertheless, no evidence has yet been forthcoming that HT, as an organization, played a direct role in radicalizing al-Hajj Dib or Hamad, although its extremist doctrines may have indirectly exerted an impact upon them.[226]

In any case, al-Hajj Dib was an Islamist fanatic who already admired the 9/11 hijackers when he first arrived in Germany, so much so that in the fall of 2004 he visited the al-Quds mosque in Hamburg, where 'Ata' and several of his fellow plotters had once prayed. Afterwards, when al-Hajj Dib returned to Kiel, he reportedly mimicked the recruitment methods adopted by the 9/11 terrorists, e.g., by organizing a prayer circle with like-minded students and making contacts with Islamists at the 'Umar ibn al-Khattab mosque on Kiel's Diedrichstrasse, a notorious meeting place for Islamist radicals that drew its ideological inspiration from the teachings of Yusuf al-Qaradawi. At that same mosque, he met German-Moroccan shop owner Ridwan al-H., an alleged al-Qa'ida courier who had links to militants in London and was reportedly entrusted with delivering messages to the ex-wife of Sa'id bin al-Hajji, a member of the Hamburg terrorist cell.[227] There are also many indications that al-Hajj Dib and Hamad were subsequently inspired by the brutal campaigns of violence carried out in Iraq by al-Zarqawi, whose al-Tawhid wa al-Jihad organization had established an elaborate support network in Europe, above all in Germany. Indeed, one of their proclaimed motives for attempting the suitcase bomb attacks was supposedly to avenge the recent death of al-Zarqawi at the hands of the Americans. There is no evidence, however, that the pair had tangible links to the Zarqawi network in Germany. Even so, the German authorities have come to believe that the attempted train bombings might have been a test of the commitment of al-Hajj Dib and Hamad, who in the event of success could have qualified themselves to participate in future al-Qa'ida missions in Iraq. The evidence cited in support of this claim was that, in an email he sent to Hamad 6 weeks before the attack, al-Hajj Dib wrote that they would need to be patient for a little longer "until we have totally made it and passed the initiation test. Then we'll travel to Iraq together."[228]

Lastly, some have suggested that the German suitcase bomb plot was covertly initiated or sponsored by a Sunni Lebanese jihadist organization called Fath al-Islam (Islamic Conquest), which broke away from a pro-Syrian jihadist group called Fath al-Intifada (Uprising Conquest) and established its base in the Nahr al-Barid Palestinian refugee camp in Beirut.[229] The reason is that Yusuf's brother Saddam al-Hajj Dib was not only a jihadist militant and a suspect in the train bombing scheme, but also a very high-ranking member of the Fath al-Islam group who was killed in May 2007 in the course of fighting against the Lebanese Army.[230] The problem with this theory is that the Fath al-Islam group appears not to have been officially established until several months *after* the summer 2006 train bombings, although it is possible that jihadist elements from earlier Lebanese organizations that later coalesced in Fath al-Islam might have played some behind-the-scenes role which is presently unclear. At the time of this writing, however, this hypothesis lacks evidentiary support.

Whatever organizational connections these two suitcase bombers might have had, it is clear from their eventual failure that none of those connections provided them with sufficient wherewithal — in the form of professional bomb-making instruction or hands-on training — to enable them to resolve the technical glitches that prevented their artisanal devices from exploding. Hence it must be assumed that the sum total of their bomb-making knowledge was derived from the aforementioned video (and perhaps other materials) that they downloaded from the Internet. In that sense, it might be irrelevant whether this particular duo did or did not constitute a genuine self-generating jihadist cell, and also whether there were other German or Lebanese members of their small group (some of whom had at various points been dubbed the "third man" and the "fourth man" by the German press), questions that cannot yet be answered with certainty. Even so, this case highlights the fact that, in lieu of at least a minimal amount of bomb-making training or experience, would-be jihadists will generally find it difficult to fabricate effective IEDs.

PART IV:

CONCLUSION

At the risk of disappointing readers, it should be emphasized at this juncture that the purpose of the above analysis has *not* been to answer definitively the question of whether small jihadist cells in the West will normally be capable of carrying out highly destructive improvised explosive device (IED) attacks or, worse still, a series of such attacks that effectively constitute a veritable IED campaign. Given the uniqueness of every case, and the varying skill and capability levels of the perpetrators who may be involved, especially with respect to IED fabrication, it is not possible to make such a general determination, much less — as social scientists often futilely presume to do — actually predict the course of future events. Hence it would be problematic, to say the least, to offer the sort of unequivocal recommendations that purport to provide an actionable guide for policymakers or intelligence personnel. In the final analysis, there are probably far too many contingent factors involved to be able to draw definitive conclusions that will be applicable in every context, so the most that one can reasonably hope to do is help illuminate and identify the crucial factors involved, not all of which will necessarily be operative in particular cases, and thereby hopefully make a small contribution to the formulation of better educated guesses about likely probabilities. (Note, moreover, that quantifying these sorts of "guesstimates" does not necessarily make them any more accurate or predictive, i.e., "scientific," despite their superficial façade of precision.) In short, the aim herein has been far more modest: to examine two recent cases of attempted IED attacks in Europe, operations which had very different results, in an effort to highlight and illustrate some of the key factors that might affect the effectiveness of future jihadist IED attacks in the West.

Yet even though no formal hypothesis testing or predictive claims are involved, a number of provisional conclusions can hopefully be drawn that may prove useful. *First, small groups of amateurs without tangible connections to experienced terrorist groups are unlikely to be able to carry out sustained campaigns of IED attacks over a significant period, even if they do successfully manage to launch one or two very destructive attacks.* In general, their built-in limitations in terms of access to resources and technical capabilities, coupled with probable deficiencies in tradecraft, will seriously inhibit their operational effectiveness, including their ability to carry out an extended series of IED attacks. In fact, such limitations might prevent them from carrying out even a single successful IED attack, as the example of the German train bombers indicates. This is not, however, a certainty, since such amateur groups might be unusually lucky or simply end up making less egregious blunders than their counterparts in the security forces. Moreover, if even one cell member happens to possess the requisite levels of bomb-making experience or expertise, the group might be able to pull off one or more bloody attacks despite its general lack of professionalism. In such a context, serendipity often plays a role.

Second, jihadist cells whose members are linked in various ways to veteran terrorist organizations, or perhaps even to experienced criminal networks, are arguably much more likely to be able to carry out successful IED attacks and campaigns than those who are members of unconnected or unaffiliated groups. This is because it is more probable in these situations that they will establish more contacts and interactions with people who can muster sufficient resources, operate well clandestinely, or perhaps even provide hands-on training in bomb making, all of which could augment their capabilities far beyond what might normally be expected.

Third, small cells that happen to include or interact directly with individuals with bomb-making experience are more likely to be able to carry out destructive IED attacks and longer-term IED campaigns. This would appear to be a self-evident proposition, though many other factors are of course also involved.

Fourth, one can never overlook the possibility that, in certain instances, lucky or talented amateurs might nonetheless succeed in launching devastating IED attacks or campaigns despite all of the odds against them, not the least of which are those related to their own likely commission of serious errors in tradecraft. The probabilities of this occurring, however, are relatively low. That is the good news.

It would be much more reassuring, from a security standpoint, if one could conclude that *only* jihadist cells made up of veteran terrorists who are linked directly and organically to wider networks would be able to carry out successful IED attacks or campaigns in Western countries. Although these connected cells, all things being equal, are surely more likely to be able to do so than small groups of amateurs, such a smug assumption would be rash and premature. Indeed, it should instead be assumed that, *in at least a few cases, amateur "bunches of guys" without any connections to foreign terrorist networks, and thus relatively deficient in terms of resources and expertise, will nevertheless succeed in perpetrating bloody mass casualty attacks with IEDs.* After all, the historical record provides examples of just such attacks. That is the bad news.

However, that same historical record has repeatedly revealed, in contradistinction to the claims of Sageman and especially Atran, that *as yet there have been very few actual examples of successful attacks, IED or otherwise, being carried out in the West by unconnected, fully autonomous cells composed entirely of amateurs.* Indeed, such a characterization of the recent and present jihadist threat is in my opinion largely a myth or, to put it another way, a "ridiculous distortion."[231] As terrorist plots planned or carried out in Britain have repeatedly illustrated, information has eventually surfaced that only serves to confirm the interconnections between local European jihadist cells and veteran terrorist organizations abroad, up to and including the provision of operational assistance by the latter to the former—despite official and unofficial initial claims to the contrary.[232] Indeed, most of the cases that have previously been cited as examples of unconnected "bottom-up" or "self-generating" jihadist groups, such as that of the Hofstadgroep (Capital City Group) in the Netherlands, do not fully conform to this overly simplistic portrayal, since if nothing else those groups usually turn out to have extensive linkages to other jihadist cells in Europe.[233] At the very least, such formulations have often been premature and exaggerated since, as has been emphasized above, most such cases in Europe have in reality been characterized by a complex combination of bottom-up and top-down processes.

ENDNOTES

1. See Committee on Defeating Improvised Explosive Devices, *Countering the Threat of Improvised Explosive Devices: Basic Research to Interrupt the IED Delivery Chain*, Washington, DC: National Academies, 2007, p. 1-1.

2. This is justly noted in *Ibid.*, p. 1-6.

3. The definition of terrorism that I have been using for the past 25 years is as follows: "the use or threatened use of violence, directed against victims selected for their symbolic or representative value, as a means of instilling anxiety in, transmitting one or more messages to, and thereby manipulating the perceptions and behavior of wider target audience(s)." In short, terrorism is nothing more than a violent technique of psychological manipulation, and like all other techniques or tactics it can be—and historically has been—employed by all sorts of protagonists and for a vast array of causes (e.g., by states, on behalf of states, and in opposition to states, by leftists, rightists, and centrists, by the religious and the irreligious, etc.). One qualification that needs to be made, however, is that the term "terrorism" should only be applied to asymmetric conflicts lest it be confused or conflated with efforts to influence wider audiences in the context of conventional military operations. Note also, in the interests of terminological precision, that the term "terror" refers to a psychological state marked by fear and anxiety, and must therefore be distinguished from terrorism. There is no such thing as a "terror network," only a "terrorist network."

4. *Countering the Threat of Improvised Explosive Devices*, p. 1-2.

5. Chris Quillen has noted that many "traditional" terrorist groups were either "not capable of or *not interested in* causing mass casualties" (italics added), an important point that needs to be kept in mind when considering the potential diffusion and adoption of improvised explosive devices (IEDs) even though "too many groups have failed to follow this tradition." See Chris Quillen, "A Historical Analysis of Mass Casualty Bombers," *Studies in Conflict and Terrorism*, Vol. 25, No. 5, 2002, p. 284.

6. As noted, the Nuclei Territoriali Antiimperialisti (NTA) did carry out several bombings, normally by placing IEDs under the parked vehicles of American servicemen. However, rather than being used to cause mass casualties or even to kill carefully selected individuals, they were instead generally detonated in the very early mornings when no one was inside the vehicles and few people were walking around, and were thus essentially intended as warnings. Yet despite its avoidance of mass casualty attacks, the NTA sought to link its own actions to those of the "fighting revolutionary vanguards that, under the guidance of the anti-imperialist Bin Laden through [their] exemplary [1998] attacks on the [African] embassies of the U.S. enemy, had known how to capitalize on years of hard work and promote the international anti-imperialist front" within the overall context of the confrontation between the forces of imperialism and anti-imperialism. The relevant excerpts from this Brigate Rosse (BR) document are cited by Gianni Cipriani, *Brigate Rosse: La minaccia del nuovo terrorismo* (*Red Brigades: The Threat of the New Terrorism*), Milan, Italy: Sperling & Kupfer, 2004, p. 253, note 40. This may have been related to the new BR's broader efforts to forge what they referred to as a "Fighting Anti-Imperialist Front" with other terrorist groups. See Otello Lupacchini, *Il ritorno delle Brigate rosse: Una sanguinosa illusione* (*The Return of the Red Brigades: A Bloody Illusion*), Rome, Italy: Koinè, 2005, pp. 239-49. It is clear that there were significant differences of opinion within this milieu about whether Islamists should be viewed as allies in the struggle.

7. See, e.g., *Qur'an* 9:73, 9:123, and 8:60 (explicit justification for terrorizing infidels).

8. Cf., e.g., *Qur'an* 2:194 and 16.126; Usama bin Ladin, October 21, 2001, interview with Taysir Alluni of al-Jazira, and an alleged member of the al-Qa'ida network in Spain, reproduced in *Messages to the World: The Statements of Osama Bin Laden*, Bruce Lawrence, ed., London, UK, and New York: Verso, 2005, p. 114; the statements by Sulayman Abu Ghayth, a Qa'idat al-Jihad spokesman who argued that Muslims have the right to kill four million Americans to compensate for the crimes and casualties allegedly perpetrated against Muslims by their "satanic" government; and pro-jihadist Saudi shaykh Nasir ibn Hamid al-Fahd, who issued a *fatwa* claiming that the use of weapons of mass destruction (WMD) against the United States to kill 10 million Americans was

justified. See, respectively, Sulayman Abu Ghayth, "In the Shade of Lances, Part I: Why We Fight America," June 12, 2002, which originally appeared on al-Qa'ida's al-Nida (The Call) website before the site was hacked and shut down, quoted in translation and available from *www.memri.org/bin/printerfriendly/pf.cgi*; and Nasir ibn Hamid al-Fahd, "Risala fi hukm istikhdam 'aslihat al-damar al-shamil didh al-kuffar" ("A Treatise on the Legal Status of Using Weapons of Mass Destruction against Infidels"), May 21, 2003, originally available from *www.al-fhd.com/rsayl/doc/rsayl.damar.doc*.

9. See, e.g., Usama bin Ladin, "Why We Are Fighting You," translated in *The Al Qaeda Reader*, Raymond Ibrahim, ed., and trans., New York: Broadway, 2007, esp. pp. 200-201; Ayman al-Zawahiri, "Jihad, Martyrdom, and the Killing of Innocents," translated in *Ibid.*, pp. 141-71. One of the arguments frequently employed by jihadists is that American civilians are legitimate targets because, by living in a democracy and voting, they are directly complicit in their elected government's "crimes" against Muslims.

10. For an emphasis on Qa'idat al-Jihad's less than fully conscious and rational or "expressive" behavioral drivers, see Jeffrey M. Bale, "Jihadist Ideology and Strategy and the Possible Employment of 'Weapons of Mass Destruction'," in *Jihadists and Weapons of Mass Destruction*, Gary Ackerman and Jeremy Tamsett, eds., New York: CRC Press, 2009, pp. 3-59. Therein I also argue that the transnational jihadists have utopian, delusional, expansionist, and frankly imperialistic agendas that cannot possibly be appeased, not—as Michael Scheuer and certain other analysts keep stubbornly insisting—defensive, limited, and pragmatic goals that are negotiable. In marked contrast, nationalist, tribally-based, and Ba'athist insurgents in countries like Iraq can be negotiated with and offered deals of various kinds, as was illustrated by the growing cooperation between elements of these groups and U.S. troops against the Tanzim Qa'idat al-Jihad fi Bilad al-Rafidayn (al-Qa'ida in Mesopotamia). On the Afghan-Pakistan frontier, there also seem to be many opportunities for making deals, at least temporarily, with tribal groups and warlords.

11. Cf., in the European context, see Lorenzo Vidino, *Al Qaeda in Europe: The New Battleground of International Jihad*, Amherst, NY: Prometheus, 2006, who emphasizes the interconnections between

wider networks and various jihadist plots in Europe, without claiming that they are centrally directed by al-Qa'ida; Marc Sageman, *Leaderless Jihad: Terror Networks in the Twenty-First Century*, Philadelphia, PA: University of Pennsylvania, 2008, who promotes the localized "bunch of guys" interpretation that he first elaborated in *Understanding Terror Networks*, Philadelphia, PA: University of Pennsylvania, 2004.

12. See, e.g., Luke Harding and Rosie Cowan, "Pakistan militants linked to London attack," *The Guardian* [London], July 19, 2005.

13. See Part III below.

14. For a relatively well-known example, see Dominique Thomas, *Le Londonistan: La voie du jihad*, Paris, France: Michalon, 2003; and Jeffrey M. Bale, "Hiding in Plain Sight in 'Londonistan,'" in Michael Innes, ed., *Denial of Sanctuary: Understanding Terrorist Safe Havens*, Westport, CT: Praeger, 2007, pp. 139-151, 192-198. In this instance, unfortunately, jihadists from throughout the Muslim world were apparently able to establish external support apparatuses in London and other British cities thanks in part to a tacit "covenant of security" that they brokered with elements of the British security services.

15. As has recently been emphasized by, e.g., Michael Kenney, *From Pablo to Osama: Trafficking and Terrorist Networks, Government Bureaucracies, and Competitive Advantage*, University Park, PA: Pennsylvania State University, 2007. See further Section II of this monograph. For evidence of learning and adaptation, see also the various jihadist "strategic" treatises that have appeared online, such as those of Abu Mus'ab al-Suri and 'Abd al-'Aziz al-Muqrin. For analyses of two of these treatises, see, respectively, Brynjar Lia, *Architect of Global Jihad: The Life of Al-Qaeda Strategist Abu Mus'ab al-Suri*, New York: Columbia University, 2008; and Norman Cigar, *Al-Qa'ida's Doctrine of Insurgency: 'Abd al-'Aziz al-Muqrin's A Practical Course for Guerrilla War*, Washington, DC: Potomac, 2009.

16. See Kenney's valuable unpublished report prepared for the U.S. Department of Justice, "Organizational Learning and Islamic Militancy," September 29, 2008, p. 34.

17. *Ibid.*, p. 21.

18. Among the first to emphasize this distinction between explicit and tacit knowledge was economic historian and philosopher Karl Polanyi in *Knowing and Being: Essays by Michael Polanyi,* Marjorie Grene, ed., Chicago, IL: University of Chicago, 1969.

19. Brian A. Jackson *et al.*, *Aptitude for Destruction, Volume 1: Organizational Learning in Terrorist Groups and its Implications for Combating Terrorism,* Santa Monica, CA: RAND, 2005, pp. 14-15.

20. *Ibid.*, p. 15.

21. For more on *techne*, see Kenney, "Organizational Learning and Islamic Militancy," pp. 6, 16-17.

22. For more on *mētis*, see *Ibid.*, pp. 6, 17-19.

23. *Ibid.*, p. 19.

24. *Ibid.*

25. Kenney, *From Pablo to Osama*, esp. chap. 5. Note, however, that most of these adaptations by terrorist organizations involve making "incremental adjustments to daily practices and tasks" rather than "substantial changes in organizational behavior," much less to the reconsideration or altering of "basic beliefs and assumptions underlying collective action." See Kenney, "Organizational Learning and Islamic Militancy," pp. 87-88; cf. also pp. 125-126.

26. Jackson *et al.*, *Aptitude for Destruction,* vol. 1, p. 9, a definition purportedly derived from that of Danny Miller, "A Preliminary Typology of Organizational Learning: Synthesizing the Literature," *Journal of Management*, Vol. 22, No. 3, 1996, pp. 485-505. However, Miller's definition (*Ibid.*, p. 486) is rather different: "the acquisition of new knowledge by actors who are able and willing to apply that knowledge in making decisions or influencing others in the organization."

27. Jackson *et al.*, *Aptitude for Destruction*, Vol. 1, p. 9 (italics mine). Moreover, the "effectiveness of a terrorist group that lacks the ability to learn will be determined *largely by chance* — the chance that its members already have the necessary skills, the chance that its current tactics are effective against desirable targets and against current countermeasures, and the chance that any accidental or arbitrary shifts the group makes will prove to be beneficial." See *Ibid.*, p. 17 (italics again mine).

28. *Ibid.*, pp. 10-14.

29. *Ibid.*, pp. 17-26.

30. *Ibid.*, p. 21.

31. It is perhaps significant that the case studies examined by these authors in Volume 2 of their study are (with one exception, the radical environmental movement), relatively large, structured, hierarchical organizations with extensive resources, viz., Aum Shinrikyo, Hizballah, Jemaah Islamiyah, and the Provisional Irish Republican Army (PIRA). See Brian A. Jackson *et al.*, *Aptitude for Destruction, Volume 2: Case Studies of Organizational Learning in Five Terrorist Groups*, Santa Monica, CA: RAND, 2005.

32. Kenney, "Organizational Learning and Islamic Militancy," p. 6. Note, however, that there is a slight but potentially important discrepancy between two diagrams presented by Kenney. In Figure 1, p. 31, a "process model of organizational learning," the process is depicted as one of acquiring, *sharing*, and applying information, whereas in Figure 2, p. 36, a "bounded process model of organizational learning," it is depicted as one of acquiring, *interpreting*, and applying ("acting upon") information. If one regards "interpreting" and "sharing" as separate processes, then Kenney's model could conceivably end up with four steps, much like that of Jackson *et al.*

33. *Ibid.*, p. 31. Therein he cites Marc Sageman and other scholars in support of this assessment. The problem, however, is that Sageman and others tend to overemphasize the importance of social networks while seriously underestimating the importance of ideological attraction in inducing individuals to join extremist groups, including those that rely primarily on terrorism as a

tactic. See Jeffrey M. Bale, "Analysis of Marc Sageman's *Leaderless Jihad*," unpublished March 2007 report prepared for components of the U.S. intelligence community, pp. 1-2, 8-11.

34. Kenney, "Organizational Learning and Islamic Militancy," p. 30. Note, however, that these three processes are not necessarily carried out in a strictly linear sequential fashion, but instead are engaged in "concurrently" and "haphazardly," since learning tends to be "fluid, messy, and subject to numerous constraints." See *Ibid.*, p. 35.

35. *Ibid.*, p. 32.

36. *Ibid.*, pp. 33-34, 101-124, 129-131.

37. *Ibid.*, p. 35.

38. *Ibid.*, pp. 35-36.

39. Here I do not mean to imply that the jihadist threat is not serious, as all too many partisan or naïve academicians have incorrectly and sometimes disingenuously claimed. For examples of works that downplay the threat of Islamist terrorism, sometimes to absurd lengths, see John Mueller, *Overblown: How Politicians and the Terrorism Industry Inflate National Security Threats, and Why We Believe Them*, New York: Simon & Schuster, 2006; John L. Esposito, *The Islamic Threat: Myth or Reality?* New York: Oxford University, 1999; Bruce B. Lawrence, *Shattering the Myth: Islam Beyond Violence*, Princeton, NJ: Princeton University, 1998; Fariba Adelkhah and Alain Gresh, eds., *Un péril islamiste? (An Islamic Threat?)*, Brussels, Belgium: Complexe, 1994; W. A. R. Shadid and P. S. van Koningsveld, *De mythe van het islamitische gevaar: Hindernissen bij intergratie (The Myth of the Islamic Threat: Obstacles to Integration)*, Kampen, Germany: J. H. Kok, 1992; and — worst of all — Emran Qureshi and Michael A. Sells, eds., *The New Crusades: Constructing the Muslim Enemy*, New York: Columbia University, 2003, a polemical work that echoes delusional jihadist propaganda. At the same time, it would also be a grave mistake to portray jihadists as uniquely-talented "super-terrorists" because: a) it is not generally true, b) it will only serve to demoralize opponents of the jihadists, and c) it will further bolster the jihadists' own, already inflated self-images and optimism about their eventual success.

40. Kenney, "Organizational Learning and Islamic Militancy," pp. 41-44. For simpler attacks, terrorist-related information in the form of *techne* is more readily available on the Internet.

41. *Ibid.*, pp. 44-45.

42. *Ibid.*, p. 45.

43. *Ibid.*, pp. 45, 49, quote. Cf. also pp. 126-127.

44. *Ibid.*, p. 50.

45. *Ibid.*, pp. 50-52.

46. *Ibid.*, p. 55.

47. *Ibid.*, pp. 55-56, e.g., in Britain experienced jihadists were intimately involved in the July 7, 2005, London bombings (Muhammad Siddiq Khan), the 2004 plot uncovered by the "Operation Crevice" counterterrorist operation ('Umar Khayyam), and the fertilizer bomb plot interdicted that same year (Dhiren Barot).

48. See *Ibid.*, pp. 57-86, wherein several examples are provided. Cf. also James Brandon, "Al-Qa'ida's Involvement in Britain's 'Homegrown' Terrorist Plots," *CTC* [Combating Terrorism Center] *Sentinel*, Vol. 2, No. 3, March 2009, pp. 10-12.

49. Vidino, *Al Qaeda in Europe*, pp. 19-51. For the European converts, see also Alison Pargeter, *The New Frontiers of Jihad: Radical Islam in Europe*, Philadelphia, PA: University of Pennsylvania Press, 2008, chap. 10.

50. It should be emphasized, however, that these "successive" stages were not always entirely discrete or fully sequential. Indeed, in many cases they were commingled chronologically. In the mid-1990s, for example, at a time when the majority of exiled jihadists in Europe were busy building support networks for groups elsewhere, some cells that were linked to the Armed Islamic Group (GIA) began carrying out a series of terrorist attacks within France.

51. See Vidino, *Al Qaeda in Europe*, pp. 43-44; Pargeter, *New Frontiers of Jihad*, pp. 1-7.

52. The same, of course, was true of many members of the Egyptian Muslim Brotherhood (MB) who had taken refuge in Europe, beginning in the 1950s but especially after Jamal 'Abd al-Nasir's harsh crackdown on the group in the 1960s. However, instead of engaging in jihadist activities, those earlier MB émigrés adopted a gradualist "Islamization from below" strategy to implant themselves institutionally, acquire religio-cultural hegemony over Muslim communities in Europe, and ultimately Islamize European host societies. See, e.g., Lorenzo Vidino, *The New Muslim Brotherhood in the West*, New York: Columbia University, 2010.

53. Lia, *Architect of Global Jihad*, esp. chaps. 2, 3, and 5.

54. Pargeter, *New Frontiers of Jihad*, chap. 4.

55. For more information on these support networks, cf. Thomas, *Londonistan*, esp. pp. 147-84; Ali Laïdi with Ahmed Salam, *Le jihad en Europe: Les filières du terrorisme islamiste* (*Jihad in Europe: The Networks of Islamist Terrorism*), Paris, France: Seuil, 2002, pp. 43-61, 169-192, 225-242; Antoine Sfeir, *Les réseaux d'Allah: La nébuleuse Ben Laden* (*The Networks of Allah: The Bin Ladin Web*), Paris, France: Plon, 2001, chap. 13; Julien Lariège, *Islamistes algériens au coeur de l'Europe: La menace djaz'ariste* (*Algerian Islamists in the Heart of Europe: The "Algerianist" Threat*), Paris, France: Ellipses, 2005; Hassane Zerrouky, *La nébuleuse islamiste en France et en Algérie* (*The Islamist Web in France and Algeria*), Paris, France: Éditions 1, 2002, pp. 104-116; Claude Moniquet, *Le djihad: Histoire secrète des hommes et des réseaux en Europe* (*Jihad: Secret History of the Persons and the Networks in Europe*), Paris, France: Ramsay, 2004, chaps. 2, 8; Mamoun Fandy, *Saudi Arabia and the Politics of Dissent,* New York: Palgrave, 1999, pp. 115-47; Sean O'Neill and Daniel McGrory, *The Suicide Factory: Abu Hamza and the Finsbury Park Mosque,* London, UK: Harper, 2006, part I; and Berndt Georg Thamm, *Terrorbasis Deutschland: Die islamistische Gefahr in unserer Mitte* (*Terrorist Base Germany: The Islamist Danger in Our Midst*), Munich, Germany: Diederichs, 2004, chap. 2.

56. See, e.g., Evan Kohlmann, *Al-Qaida's Jihad in Europe: The Afghan-Bosnian Network*, New York: Berg, 2004, esp. chap. 9.

57. See, e.g., Vidino, *Al Qaeda in Europe*, pp. 135-136, 140-142, 147, 172-175.

58. On 9/11, see National Commission on Terrorist Attacks Upon the United States, *Final Report*, Washington, DC: Government Printing Office, 2002; and Terry McDermott, *Perfect Soldiers. The 9/11 Hijackers: Who They Were, Why They Did It*, New York: Harper, 2005.

59. Among these actions was the assassination 2 days before 9/11, of anti-Taliban Afghan commander Ahmad Shah Mas'ud. See, e.g., Jean-Marie Pontaut and Marc Epstein, *Ils ont assassiné Massoud: Révélations sur l'International terroriste* (*Massoud Has Been Assassinated: Revelations about the Terrorist International*), Paris, France: Robert Laffont, 2002, a "martyrdom" operation carried out by, among others, jihadists based in Belgium. See also Vidino, *Al Qaeda in Europe*, Part II, who provides an excellent overview of the many terrorist plots and actions in Europe attributed to Algerian networks during this period.

60. *Ibid.*, chap. 11; Pargeter, *New Frontiers of Jihad*, chaps. 8-9.

61. This interpretation has been promoted by Marc Sageman in two influential books, *Understanding Terror Networks* and, with even more force, *Leaderless Jihad*. For similar claims, expressed even more categorically, see Olivier Roy, "Al Qaeda: A True Global Movement," in *Jihadi Terrorism and the Radicalisation Challenge in Europe*, Rik Coolsaet, ed., Aldershot, UK, and Burlington, VT: Ashgate, 2008, p. 113: "Al Qaeda is not a centralized, hierarchical, Leninist type of organisation. [Author's note: This is a straw man, since no one has ever claimed that it was.] It now consists of bottom-up networks." Sageman and others, e.g., Jason Burke, are in effect arguing that al-Qa'ida is less an actual organization and more the high-profile figurehead or voice of a diffuse "social movement." However, I have argued elsewhere that it is very problematic to characterize al-Qa'ida's sympathizers as a "social movement," which suggests a much more structured, mass-based, or explicitly articulated worldwide phenomenon than is presently observable. In my opinion al-Qa'ida instead constitutes

the principal organizational expression, effectively the self-styled vanguard (*tali'a*), of a globally-oriented jihadist Salafist ideological milieu that is focused on targeting the "far enemy," i.e., the United States and its Western allies. See Bale, "Analysis of Marc Sageman's *Leaderless Jihad*," pp. 10-11.

62. Bruce Hoffman, "The Myth of Grass-Roots Terrorism: Why Osama bin Laden Still Matters," *Foreign Affairs*, Vol. 87, No. 3, May-June 2008, pp. 133-138.

63. *Ibid.*, esp. pp. 134-135.

64. See, e.g., the publicly released summary of the June 21, 2007, National Intelligence Estimate (NIE), National Intelligence Council, "The Terrorist Threat to the US Homeland," p. 6, available from *www.c-span.org/pdf/nie_071707.pdf*, which emphasizes that al-Qa'ida "is and will remain the most serious terrorist threat to the homeland," and that its "central leadership continues to plan high-impact plots" and "enhance its capabilities...through greater cooperation with regional terrorist groups." However, the report also warns (*Ibid.*, p. 7) of the "growing number of radical, self-generating cells in Western countries." Cf. also former intelligence officer Bruce Riedel, "Al Qaeda Strikes Back," *Foreign Affairs*, Vol. 86, No. 3, May-June 2007, p. 24, which begins as follows: "Al Qaeda is a more dangerous enemy today than it has ever been before."

65. Marc Sageman, "The Reality of Grass-Roots Terrorism," *Foreign Affairs*, July-August 2008, pp. 163-165; and "The Homegrown Young Radicals of Next-Gen Jihad," *Washington Post*, June 8, 2008.

66. Will McCants, "Smackdown! Sageman vs. Hoffman," Jihadica website, June 8, 2008, available from *www.jihadica.com/smackdown-sageman-vs-hoffman/*.

67. See the comments of several interviewees, including U.S. Defense Secretary Robert Gates and European judges and investigators, in Elaine Sciolino and Eric Schmitt, "A Not Very Private Feud Over Terrorism," *New York Times*, June 8, 2008. Cf. also the account of their feud by Stephen Tankel, "The Hoffman-Sageman

Dustup Goes Mainstream," Kings of War website, June 8, 2008, available from *kingsofwar.wordpress.com/2008/06/08/the-hoffman-%E2%80%93-sageman-dustup-goes-mainstream/*.

68. As Phil Williams rightly notes in "In Cold Blood: The Madrid Bombings," *Perspectives on Terrorism*, June 2008, a special issue on "Under-Investigated Topics in Terrorism Research," p. 19. He goes on to add that "in a complex world, the integration of multiple models is likely to offer a much closer approximation to reality than models which claim exclusivity and universality."

69. To be more precise, al-Qa'ida is relatively small by comparison to many insurgent organizations, but rather large by comparison to most terrorist organizations.

70. This is somewhat misleading, however, insofar as it suggests that the other committees of the *majlis al-shura* are concerned primarily with "nonmilitary" affairs. In fact, what the military committee is concerned with are operational matters, whereas the financial committee and training committees are both concerned with logistical matters and the so-called *fatwa* committee is concerned with evaluating the religious appropriateness of the tangible actions to be undertaken by the group. For the general organizational structure of al-Qa'ida and its *majlis al-shura* before 9/11, see the February 6, 2001, testimony of high-ranking Sudanese insider Jamal al-Fadl in United States District Court, Southern District of New York, *USA v. Usama bin Laden* (S, 7) 98 Cr. 1023, February 6, 2001, pp. 204-211. Cf. Devin R. Springer, James L. Regens, and David N. Edger, *Islamic Radicalism and Global Jihad*, Washington, DC: Georgetown University Press, 2009, pp. 103-107, esp. Figure 3.4, p. 105. There is every reason to believe, however, that Bin Ladin's group still retains its *majlis al-shura* structure despite its post-U.S. invasion flight from Afghanistan into Pakistan. It is primarily beneath that upper leadership level that the greatest organizational changes have since occurred, probably less for abstract theoretical reasons than for purely practical reasons. Hence the claims by some observers that al-Qa'ida has since officially adopted Abu Mus'ab al-Suri's networked "leaderless resistance" model are premature, since they not only exaggerate the influence of the Syrian jihadist strategic thinker on Bin Ladin and his closest collaborators, but also minimize the influence of other jihadist theoreticians who have advocated consolidation rather than decentralization. See the discussion in *Ibid.*, pp. 108-131.

71. The precise number of rank-and-file members has fluctuated considerably over time, and probably reached its lowest ebb after the U.S. military and its Afghan allies toppled the Taliban regime and drove the surviving al-Qa'ida fighters across the Afghan frontier into the Pashtun tribal zones of Pakistan.

72. See, e.g., Springer *et al.*, *Islamic Radicalism and Global Jihad*, pp. 102-103. This has in turn produced friction between members from different nationalities and ethnicities, generating internal divisions and fissures that counterterrorist forces should be exacerbating or otherwise exploiting. See, e.g., Fawaz A. Gerges, *Far Enemy: Why Jihad Went Global,* Cambridge, UK: Cambridge University Press, 2005, esp. pp. 101-109; al-Fadl testimony in *USA v. Usama bin Laden*, February 7, 2001, pp. 321-324.

73. Bin Ladin's obsession with the apostasy of the Saudi regime and its ongoing persecution of radicals is frequently reflected in his public statements. Likewise, to this day al-Zawahiri is engaged in polemics with former jihadist comrades in Egypt over tactics and their decision to renounce violent struggle. See, e.g., his bitter polemics with Muntasir al-Zayyat, which can in part be followed by comparing Montasser al-Zayyat, *The Road to Al-Qaeda: The Story of Bin Laden's Right-Hand Man,* London, UK: Pluto, 2004, especially chaps. 4-8; and al-Zawahiri, *Fursan tahta rayat al-nabi'* (*Knights under the Prophet's Banner*), serialized in *Al-Sharq al-Awsat* in December 2001, parts 8-9. Compare also Gerges, *Far Enemy*, especially chaps. 3 and 4.

74. See, e.g., Jason Burke, *Al Qaeda: Casting a Shadow of Terror,* London, UK: I. B. Taurus, 2003, pp. 7-22; Erik Schechter, "Generic Jihad," *Jerusalem Post*, December 5, 2003; and Jerry Mark Long, "Strategic Culture, al-Qaida, and Weapons of Mass Destruction," Science Applications International Corporation (SAIC) report prepared for the Defense Threat Reduction Agency, November 20, 2006, pp. 3-4.

75. However, it is now clear that some of the July 7, 2005 (7/7), London bombing plotters received specialized training at jihadist camps in Pakistan run by Lashkar-i Tayyiba, a group with close links to al-Qa'ida Central. Hence it is highly misleading to characterize this cell as an autonomous "self-starter" group composed of amateurs, as it is with many other United Kingdom (UK) and Europe-based cells. For more on the 7/7 bomb-

ings, see the official report by the British authorities, House of Commons, Intelligence and Security Committee, *Report of the Official Account of the Bombings in London on 7 July 2005, 11 May 2006*, London, UK: Stationery Office, 2006. See further O'Neill and McGrory, *Suicide Factory*, esp. pp. 269-76; Crispin Black, *7/7, the London Bombs: What went Wrong?* London, UK: Gibson Square, 2005; and Nafeez Mossadeq Ahmed, *The London Bombings: An Independent Inquiry*, Woodstock, NY: Overlook, 2006, which, despite the author's political biases, provides much useful material.

76. For examples of Bin Ladin's public and indeed proud claims to function as an instigator of jihadist terrorism, see Bruce Lawrence, ed., *Messages to the World: The Statements of Osama Bin Laden*, London, UK, and New York: Verso, 2005, pp. 69, where he says it is his duty is to motivate the umma to wage jihad against the United States, Israel, and their allies, and pp. 107-108, where he admits that he incited "martyrs" to carry out the September 11, 2001 (9/11), attacks in "self-defense," as well as inciting other attacks on Americans and Jews, which is a religious duty, and says that if this makes him a terrorist, so be it.

77. See, respectively, Mark Mazzetti and Scott Shane, "Bin Laden was active in planning attacks," *New York Times*, May 6, 2011; and Syed Saleem Shahzad, *Inside Al Qaida and the Taliban: Beyond Bin Laden and 9/11*, London, UK: Pluto, 2011.

78. Javier Jordán, Fernando M. Mañas, and Nicola Horsburgh, "Strengths and Weaknesses of Grassroots Jihadist Networks: The Madrid Bombings," *Studies in Conflict and Terrorism*, Vol. 31, 2008, pp. 18-19. Others have referred to these latter types of cells using slightly different but comparable terms, e.g., as "self-generating" or "freelance" jihadist groups or as "local autonomous cells and networks." See, respectively, Springer *et al.*, *Islamic Radicalism and Global Jihad*, pp. 132-133, 164-166, in the context of recruitment and radicalization; and Algemene Inlichtingen-en Veiligheidsdienst (General Intelligence and Security Service [AIVG]), *Violent Jihad in the Netherlands: Current Trends in the Islamist Terrorist Threat*, The Hague, The Netherlands: AIVD Communications Department, 2006, esp. pp. 37-39. Whatever terminology is employed, these cells purportedly "lack direct links to al-Qa'ida Central but rely on the same overall strategy and shared goals." See Springer *et al.*, *Islamic Radicalism and Global Jihad*, p. 139.

79. E.g., it is currently very difficult to obtain trial materials dealing with jihadist plots in many European countries, including France, Belgium, Germany, and the UK. The short official reports that are sometimes made available, such as the reports on the 7/7 bombing, generally lack sufficient detail to permit detailed reconstructions of the events, in particular the systematic tracing of linkages between members of the implicated networks.

80. Ironically, the definition provided in a Wikipedia article on which the above definition is based seems vastly preferable to the original definition provided by J. A. Barnes in the 1950s, "[a]n association of people drawn together by family, work, or hobby."

81. "Social Network Analysis: A Brief Introduction," undated, available from *www.orgnet.com/sna.html*.

82. *Ibid.*

83. See, e.g., Valdis E. Krebs, "Uncloaking Terrorist Networks," *First Monday*, Vol. 7, No. 4, April 1, 2002, available from *firstmonda .org/htbin/cgiwrap/bin/ojs/index.php/fm/article/view /941/863*; "Social Network Analysis of the 9/11 Terrorist Network," 2002, available from *www.orgnet.com/hijackers.html*; "Connecting the Dots: Tracking Two Identified Terrorists," 2002 (but with more recent updates), available from *www.orgnet.com/tnet. html*; Justin Magouik, Scott Atran, and Marc Sageman, "Connecting Terrorist Networks," *Studies in Conflict and Terrorism*, Vol. 31, No. 1, 2008, pp. 1-16; and Jordán *et al.*, "Grassroots Jihadist Networks." For a more skeptical perspective on the efficacy of social network analysis (SNA), one which in my opinion is largely justified, see Patrick Radden Keefe, "Can Network Theory Thwart Terrorists?" *New York Times*, March 12, 2006, available from *www. nytimes.com/2006/03/12/magazine/312wwln_essay.html?_r=1*.

84. That is why we historians sometimes sardonically quip that the only way the future can be accurately predicted is retrospectively.

85. For these details, cf. the accounts in Administración de Justicia, Juzgado Central de Instrucción No. 6, Audencia Nacional, Madrid, Sumario No. 20/2004, *Auto de procesamiento* (*Indict-*

ment), April 10, 2006 (hereafter *Auto 10/04/06*), pp. 1-6, 47-74, 110-113; Administración de Justicia, Juzgado Central de Instrucción No. 6, Audencia Nacional, Madrid, Spain, Sumario No. 20/2004, *Declaración del Fiscal (Public Prosecutor's Statement*), November 7, 2006 (hereafter *Declaración 07/11/06*), pp. 46-60; Administración de Justicia, Juzgado Central de Instrucción No. 6, Audencia Nacional, Madrid, Sumario No. 20/2004, *Sentencia (contra Jamal Zougam + 28) (Sentence) número 65/2007*, July 31, 2007 (hereafter *Sentencia 31/07/07*), pp. 172-177; and Casimiro García-Abadillo, *11-M: La venganza*, Madrid, Spain: Esfera de los Libros, 2004, pp. 16-30.

86. *Auto 10/04/06*, pp. 132-141.

87. *Auto 10/04/06*, pp. 144-61; *Declaración 07/11/06*, pp. 95-9; *Sentencia 31/07/07*, pp. 177-181.

88. *Auto 10/04/06*, pp. 130-2; *Declaración 07/11/06*, pp. 101-109.

89. *Declaración 07/11/06*, pp. 109-10; García-Abadillo, *11-M*, pp. 106-107. This particular shop was run by an Indian named Rakesh Kumar and co-owned by his brother Suresh Kumar and Vinay Kholi. The former and Kholi were also the co-owners of Sindhu Enterprise, the store that had sold the SIM cards to Zugham's Siglo Nuevo shop. Also of potential significance is that Rakesh had paid Ayman Mawsili Kalaji, the owner of the Test Ayman mobile phone shop, located at Calle Santa María de la Cabeza 177, to change the codes of 12 of those phones so that they would accept a different SIM card. Curiously, Kalaji was also a Spanish policeman who at one point had served as a bodyguard for anti-terrorist judge Baltasar Garzón, which later provided fuel for several conspiracy theorists, who were claiming that the 3/11 attacks were a state-sponsored "false flag" terrorist operation. For more on Kalaji, see Fernando Mugica, "El policía que preparó las bombas?" ("The Policeman who prepared the bombs?"), *El Mundo*, August 22, 2005, available from *kickjor.blogspot.com/2005/08/los-agujeros-negros-del-11-m-xxi-el.html*.

90. *Declaración 07/11/06*, pp. 110-120; *Sentencia 31/07/07*, pp. 184-189.

91. For the information on this video cassette, see *Declaración 07/11/06*, pp. 87-89.

92. However, the jihad name Abu Dujan[a] al-Afghani may actually have been the moniker of a logistical operative of the Groupe Islamique Combattant Marocain (GICM) based in Belgium named Yusuf ibn al-Hajj. See *Ibid.*, p. 69. The term *ansar*, meaning "partisans," "helpers," or "supporters," has a special significance in Islamic history since it originally referred to Muhammad's earliest followers in Medina, in contradistinction to the dedicated companions from Mecca who accompanied him on the *hijra* or "emigration" to Medina, who are instead known as the *muhajirun* or "émigrés." Hence one now finds that many jihadist groups incorporate the terms *ansar* or *muhajirun* into their names. The name "Abu Dujan" was probably derived from that of Abu Dujana, an especially brave companion of Muhammad's who was particularly skilled in using weapons in melees and who distinguished himself at the Battle of Uhud (625 CE).

93. *Ibid.*, p. 89. A reproduction of two shots from that video cassette appear in García-Abadillo, *11-M*, on the third page of illustrations following p. 128.

94. *Declaración 07/11/06*, pp. 90-91. For an analysis of the Abu Hafs al-Masri Brigades statement, see Yigal Carmon, "The Alleged Al-Qa'ida Statement of Responsibility for the Madrid Bombings: Translation and Commentary," MEMRI website, Inquiry and Analysis #166, March 12, 2004, available from *www.memri.org/bin/latestnews.cgi?ID=IA16604*. Note that the Abu Hafs al-Masri Brigades were named after the "jihad name" of Egyptian militant Muhammad 'Atif, one of Usama bin Ladin's chief lieutenants and the head of the Military Committee of al-Qa'ida's *majlis al-shura* prior to his death in an American air strike in 2001. This particular group has often claimed responsibility for jihadist attacks in the West, but it is unclear (and perhaps doubtful) whether it is a real organization and, if so, whether it is, in fact, linked to al-Qa'ida. Note further that in an October 2003 videotape (which the CIA considered authentic), Bin Ladin had explicitly included Spain in a list of countries that could be legitimately attacked by jihadists.

95. In 2002, Centro Superior de Información de la Defensa (CESID) was renamed the Central Nacional de Inteligencia (National Intelligence Center [CNI]).

96. For the information in this paragraph, see José Maria Irujo, *El agujero: España invadida por la yihad (The Opening: Spain Invaded by the Jihad)*, Madrid: Santillana, 2005, pp. 64-65, 148, 243-244, 332-335; and García-Abadillo, *11-M*, pp. 91-95.

97. For the information in this paragraph, see *Ibid.*, pp. 95-101.

98. For this call, see further Irujo, *Agujero*, pp. 346-348.

99. Ironically, the day before, several of the terrorists and their families had been at that very site to attend a party, and had then (unsuccessfully) tried to remove traces of their activities before leaving to take refuge elsewhere. See *Ibid.*, pp. 351-352.

100. For the materials found therein, see *Auto 10/04/06*, pp. 204-208.

101. García-Abadillo, *11-M*, pp. 177-178.

102. *Auto 10/04/06*, pp. 161-163. The investigators concluded that if this bomb had been detonated when a high-speed train was passing, it could have resulted in the deaths of more people than the 3/11 attacks. A few days earlier, near midnight on March 30, Red Nacional de Ferrocarriles Españoles (RENFE) employees had interrupted five men digging a hole under the Alta Velocidad Española (AVE) tracks on the Madrid-Lérida line, near the juncture of Mercamadrid, but the culprits fled and escaped. Later, the police became convinced that they were the same individuals who subsequently placed the bomb under the Madrid-Seville AVE line. García-Abadillo, *11-M*, p. 200.

103. For the "siege" of the Leganés apartment, cf. *Ibid.*, pp. 201-207; Irujo, *Agujero*, pp. 356-364; Manuel Marlasca and Luis Rendueles, *Una historia del 11-M que no va a gustar a nadie (A History of 3/11 That Will Make No One Happy)*, Madrid, Spain: Temas de Hoy, 2007, pp. 76-88; and *Sentencia 31/07/07*, pp. 204-206.

104. For the forensic evidence from Leganés, see *Auto 10/04/06*, pp. 163-193; *Declaración 07/11/06*, pp. 152-165; and *Sentencia 31/07/07*, pp. 206-212.

105. Cf., e.g., "Madrid Victims Attack 'Leniency,'" BBC website, November 1, 2007, available from *news.bbc.co.uk/2/hi/europe/7071990.stm*; Soeren Kern, "Spain Faces Difficulties in Judging Islamic Terrorists," Power and Interest News Report website, November 12, 2007, available from *www.pinr.com/report.php?ac=view_report&report_id=719&language_id=1*; and Lisa Abend, "Deep Divisions over Madrid Verdict," *Christian Science Monitor*, November 1, 2007, available from *www.csmonitor.com/2007/1101/p07s02-woeu.html*.

106. See the short summary of the sentences meted out in José María de Pablo, *La cuarta trama: Verdades y mentiras en el caso del 11-M* (*The Fourth Plot: Truths and Lies in the 3/11 Case*), Madrid, Spain: Ciudadela, 2009, pp. 20-21, notes 7-9.

107. For the view that the Madrid cell was in various important ways connected to broader jihadist networks, including those linked to al-Qa'ida, see Vidino, *Al Qaeda in Europe*, pp. 295-340; Irujo, *Agujero*; J. A. Emerson Vermaat, "The Madrid Terrorism Trial Verdict—Some Critical Comments," Militant Islam Monitor website, November 18, 2007, available from *www.militantislammonitor.org/article/id/3256*; and Luis de la Corte Ibáñez and Javier Jordán, *La yihad terrorista* (*The Terrorist Jihad*), Madrid, Spain: Síntesis, 2007, pp. 246-253. For the Madrid bombings as the product of an essentially local cell, see Daniel Benjamin and Steven Simon, *The Next Attack: The Failure of the War on Terror and a Strategy for Getting it Right,* New York: Henry Holt, 2005, pp. 3-16; and Scott Atran and Marc Sageman, "The Great Train Bombing," preliminary draft report, October 10, 2007, pp. 5-12, and *passim* (previously, but no longer) available from *www.healthsystem.virginia.edu/internet/ciag/london/Madrid-Bombing-10Oct07.pdf*.

108. For an illustration of the latter group's perspective, see Jason Burke, "What role did al-Qaida play?" *The Guardian* [London], October 31, 2007, available from *www.guardian.co.uk/commentisfree/2007/oct/31/whatroledidalqaidaplay*; and the revealing comments made by Scott Atran in the course of an interview with a reporter from *The Guardian*:

> There isn't the slightest bit of evidence of any operational relationship with al-Qaida. . . . The overwhelming majority of [ter-

rorist cells] in Europe have nothing to do with al-Qaida other than a vague relationship of ideology. And even that ideology is fairly superficial—it's basically a reaction to what they see as a war on Islam around the world. . . . These young men [the Madrid bombers] radicalised themselves.

Cited in Paul Hamilos, "The Worst Islamist Attack in European History," *Guardian*, October 31, 2007, available from *www.guardian.co.uk/world/2007/oct/31/spain*. Only if one defines the word "operational" in its narrowest possible sense, can one claim that there are no al-Qa'ida links to the 3/11 cell. Furthermore, as will become clearer below, I disagree strongly with his last two quoted conclusions. Although Atran and I do agree that the trial of the 3/11 bombers was a "farce," we do so for entirely opposing reasons.

109. See *Declaración 07/11/06*, pp. 21-26, a section headed "Formation of the Terrorist Cell: [The] Group that Executed the Attack and [the] Group of Jamal Ahmidan." Cf. also the title of chap. 3 in Marlasca and Rendueles, *Una historia del 11-M* (*A History of 3/11*), "The Tunisian and the Chinaman: The Mind and the Muscle." Another interesting scheme has been proposed by a lawyer representing the Asociación de Ayuda a las Víctimas del 11-M (Support Association for 3/11 Victims). See De Pablo, *Cuarta trama*, part 2. De Pablo identifies three plots or conspiracies—one involving Spanish criminals in Asturias to sell illicit goods, including explosives; a second involving a group of Arab criminals led by Jamal Ahmidan, to obtain explosives; and a third involving the members of a jihadist cell headed by Fakhit, who wanted to carry out bombings. Still another petty criminal named Rafa Zuhayr acted as an intermediary in bringing the three groups together. However, despite providing a wealth of interesting details based upon a close examination of the voluminous trial materials, the general value of De Pablo's book is undermined by his improbable partisan claim that there was a "fourth plot" involving Euskadi ta Askatasuna (ETA) and others to bring the Partido Socialista Obrero Español (Spanish Socialist Workers' Party [PSOE]) to power by staging a terrorist attack that could be blamed on jihadists.

110. *Declaración 07/11/06*, pp. 21-23.

111. *Ibid.*, pp. 23-26.

112. See Table 2 in Irujo, *Agujero*, p. 390. However, in 2001 Fakhit was not yet considered sufficiently important by Judge Garzón to be arrested or charged in the indictment he issued against the network. See García-Abadillo, *11-M*, p. 109.

113. Al-Shadadi, al-Shabli, and Nidal all appeared in the list of the accused in the final sentence against members of the Abu Dahdah network. See Administración de Justicia, Juzgado Central de Instrucción No. 5, Audencia Nacional, Madrid, Spain, Sumario No. 35/01, *Sentencia* (*contra Imad Eddin Barakat Yarkas + 23*), September 26, 2005 (hereafter *Sentencia 26/09/05*), pp. 3, 5. In the earlier indictment, charges were filed against both al-Shadadi and al-'Azizi. See Administración de Justicia, Juzgado Central de Instrucción No. 5, Audencia Nacional, Madrid, Spain, Sumario No. 35/01, *Auto de procesamiento*, September 17, 2003 (hereafter *Auto 17/09/03*), pp. 1-2.

114. For this GICM-al-Qa'ida pact, based on the statements of Nafi'yya himself, see "Probe of London Attacks Targets a Network of Radicals in Europe," *Wall Street Journal*, July 11, 2005.

115. Indeed, in March 2002 the Comisaría General de Información (General Intelligence Commissariat [CGI]), the intelligence arm of the Cuerpo Nacional de Policía (National Police Corps [CNP]), made the startling announcement that Spain was the primary al-Qa'ida base in Europe. See Irujo, *Agujero*, p. 19.

116. It remains unclear just how central a role Abu Mus'ab al-Suri played in the Spanish al-Qa'ida network. Irujo describes him as "the founder" of the "cell" in Spain, whereas Lia provides a more nuanced assessment. Cf. *Ibid.*, p. 50; and Lia, *Architect of Global Jihad*, pp. 137-142, 146-147. There is no doubt, however, that he was a close collaborator of Abu Dahdah, since Spanish police who were keeping them under surveillance documented their interactions. See, e.g., *Auto 17/09/03*, pp. 26-29, 93; Irujo, *Agujero*, pp. 23-25.

117. *Auto 17/09/03*, pp. 23-24, 63-64, etc.;

118. These linkages between Abu Dahdah and his lieutenants and other jihadist networks have been exhaustively documented in *Auto 17/09/03*. See also Lia, *Architect of Global Jihad*, pp. 142-146.

119. For more details about the 'Ata' and al-Shayb visit to Spain in July 2001, cf. *Auto 17/09/03*, pp. 317-330; National Commission on Terrorist Attacks Upon the United States, *Final Report*, Washington, DC: Government Printing Office, 2002, pp. 244-246. According to the first of the above sources (pp. 317-322), 'Ata' arrived in Madrid from Miami via Zurich on July 9, rented a room in the Hotel Diana Cazadora near Madrid's Baraja airport, and picked up a rental car the following day. Between July 9 and 13, there is no record of where he went or who he met with. From July 13 to 15, he rented a room at the Hotel Sant Jordi on Via Augusta in Tarragona, southwest of Barcelona, very close to Reus, a town where al-Shayb stayed after arriving in Barcelona on a flight from Hamburg on July 9. On the night of July 16-17, the same night al-Shayb flew back to Germany, 'Ata' rented a room at the Hotel Casablanca Playa on Paseo del Mar 12 in the nearby town of Salou, where he also rented rooms in two other hotels the next 2 nights. On July 19, 'Ata' flew from Madrid to Fort Lauderdale via Atlanta.

120. *Auto 17/09/03*, pp. 320-321, 324-330. The remaining information in this paragraph derives from this source. Cf. also Irujo, *Agujero*, pp. 80-84; and Marlasca and Rendueles, *Una historia del 11-M*, p. 121.

121. *Auto 17/09/03*, p. 88. For these conversations between Abu Dahdah and Shakur, see pp. 87-89, 330-336. The only thing odd here is that the phrase is in the past perfect tense, as if the actions described had already taken place.

122. Note that in Spain, the more important jihadist networks were normally headed by relatively well-educated and socially privileged Syrians, most of whom had been forced to seek refuge abroad after being subjected to harsh Ba'athist repression at home due to their membership in the Muslim Brotherhood. The rank and file members of those networks, on the other hand, tended to be composed of relatively poor and uneducated individuals from North Africa, especially Morocco. Fakhit was somewhat unique inasmuch as he was a privileged North African who ended up joining jihadist groups based in Spain.

123. For the information in this paragraph on Fakhit's background, cf. García-Abadillo, *11-M*, pp. 107-108; Marlasca and Rendueles, *Una historia del 11-M*, pp. 105-122; and Justin Webster and Ignacio Orovio, *Conexión Madrid: Cómo y por qué Sarhane y Jamal se convirtieron en terroristas yihadistas* (*Madrid Connection: How and Why Sarhane and Jamal Became Jihadist Terrorists*), Barcelona, Spain: Debate, 2009, pp. 32-49.

124. In the words of García-Abadillo, *11-M*, p. 108. Cf. the account in Webster and Orovio, *Conexión Madrid*, pp. 70-84.

125. For the growing schism between Fakhit and his new "brothers" and the M-30 imam, see *Ibid.*, pp. 105-117. One symbol of this was a public incident outside the mosque involving al-'Azizi, who openly expressed contempt for both the imam and the Arab leaders who were visiting the M-30 mosque to pay their respects on the occasion of the death of Syrian Ba'athist leader Hafiz al-Asad in June 2000.

126. Marlasca and Rendueles, *Una historia del 11-M*, p. 117.

127. Webster and Orovio, *Conexión Madrid*, pp. 116-117.

128. Given that al-Maymuni was a key member of a Moroccan jihadist group with an almost identical name — al-Salafiyya al-Jihadiyya — it is probably not a coincidence that he chose that name for the Spanish cell-in-formation. In actual fact, the term refers to an Islamist ideological current known as jihadist Salafism, which has been the dominant ideology espoused by many of the most radical Islamist ideologues and activists in recent decades, including Sayyid Qutub and Usama bin Ladin. For this and other reasons, there is some question about whether that appellation actually refers to a structured jihadist organization or to a loose network of autonomous cells composed of like-minded militants in Morocco. On the other hand, some have suggested that it may be little more than a front for the GICM. Though this is not certain, the GICM, which was established in the early 1990s by 'Abd al-Karim al-Majati and other Moroccan veterans of the Afghan jihad, apparently claimed kinship with Salafiyya Jihadiyya — the current and/or the organization. See Mathieu Guidère, *Al-Qaïda à la conquête du Maghreb: Le terrorisme aux portes de l'Europe* (*Al Qaida Seeking to Conquer North Africa: Terrorism at the Doors of*

Europe), Monaco: Rocher, 2007, p. 188. For more on this Moroccan al-Salafiyya al-Jihadiyya group, current, or tendency, see Ahmed Chaarani, *La mouvance islamiste au Maroc: Du 11 septembre 2001 aux attentats de Casablanca du 16 mai 2003* (*The Islamist Movement in Morocco: From 9/11 to the Casablanca Attacks of 16 May 2003*), Paris, France: Karthala, 2004, pp. 194-216. Chaarani also suggests (*Ibid.*, p. 129) that this name, which was first supposedly coined by the Moroccan secret services, was indiscriminately applied to militants who were actually members of the Moroccan branch of al-Takfir wa al-Hijra (Excommunication and Migration), for which see *Ibid.*, pp. 129-143.

129. *Ibid.*, pp. 125-130. This does not mean, of course, that the Iraq War served as the primary motivation behind, much less the underlying "cause" of, the 3/11 bombings, as many have naively argued. On the contrary, the February 2003 American invasion simply provided a new "hot button" issue that served to anger Muslims, which the jihadists could then easily exploit in order to recruit new followers and rationalize attacks on "infidels" in the former Muslim territory of al-Andalus. However, the Islamists have never accepted the fact that al-Andalus had fallen permanently under the control of the "Crusaders," and consequently they have long been obsessed with re-conquering it for Islam. For the ideological background of jihadist animosity toward Spain, see Gustavo de Arístegui, *La Yihad en España: La obsesión por reconquistar Al-Andalus* (*Jihad in Spain: The Obsession with Reconquering Al-Andalus*), Madrid, Spain: Esfera de los Libros, 2005, esp. chap. 3. Cf. also Serafín Fanjul, *La quimera de Al-Andalus* (*The Al-Andalus Fantasy*), Madrid, Spain: Siglo XXI, 2004. Moreover, as one journalist accurately noted about those particular jihadists, which also applies to other global jihadists, "They hate Europe and everything it represents." See León King, *Marruecos: La amenaza. Su guerra de baja cota contra España* (*Morocco, the Menace: Its Low Intensity Warfare against Spain*), Barcelona, Spain: Pyre, 2005, p. 203. Cf. Mary Habeck, *Knowing the Enemy: Jihadist Ideology and the War on Terror*, New Haven, CT: Yale University, 2007, chap. 4.

130. Irujo, *Agujero*, pp. 170, 198, 244.

131. For photographs of these locales, see Atran and Sageman, "Great Train Bombing," pp. 41-45. In that article, they also provide a very valuable service by visually depicting the devel-

opmental evolution of the components of the 3/11 cell, noting the individuals who joined and left at various junctures. See *Ibid.*, pp. 30-69.

132. García-Abadillo, *11-M*, pp. 108-109.

133. Marlasca and Rendueles, *Una historia del 11-M*, pp. 113-118.

134. *Ibid.*, pp. 113-122.

135. *Ibid.*, pp. 118-119, 123-132.

136. *Ibid.*, p. 131. The best short summary of the information provided by "Cartagena" can be found in De Pablo, *Cuarta trama*, pp. 69-77.

137. García-Abadillo, *11-M*, pp. 113-115.

138. For the information in this paragraph, see *Ibid.*, pp. 91-93.

139. Cf. also Marlasca and Rendueles, *Una historia del 11-M*, pp. 46-47.

140. Sa'id al-Shadadi may be of special importance with respect to IEDs, given that in the course of searching his apartment, the police found a notebook in which he had sketched a diagram for fabricating bombs using mobile phones as timers. Note also that in front of his apartment, located on Calle Caravaca, was the Rebiz Moda shop owned by Sheng-hua Huang, where the 3/11 plotters purchased the sports bags and backpacks that were later used to carry and conceal the train bombs. See García-Abadillo, *11-M*, p. 93.

141. See *Ibid.*, pp. 93-95, for the following information.

142. For brief accounts of Courtailler and his planned terrorist activities, see "Frenchman Jailed Over Terror Ties," BBC News, May 25, 2004; and Peter Graff and John Boyle, "An Islamic Militant's Odyssey," Reuters, May 20, 2004.

143. García-Abadillo, *11-M*, p. 94. Some have claimed, in contrast, that Zugham had been only a peripheral figure in the Abu Dahdah cell. See Williams, "In Cold Blood," p. 21. My own view is that the truth lies somewhere between these polar interpretations, since it is clear that Zugham had become increasingly close to Abu Dahdah, and thus less and less peripheral, in the period prior to the latter's arrest.

144. *Ibid*. Indeed, the Moroccan police informed their Spanish counterparts — *after* the 3/11 attacks — that Zugham and his associates were "dangerous jihadists" who were members of the GICM, the group they claimed was responsible for the 2003 Casablanca bombings. See King, *Marreucos*, p. 206. For more background information on Mullah Krikar, see Trevor Stanley, "Mullah Krekar: Leader of Kurdish Ansar al-Islam," Perspectives on World History and Current Events website, 2005, available from *www.pwhce.org/krekar.html*.

145. For more on Fizazi, cf. Malika Zeghal, *Les islamistes marocains: Le défi à la monarchie (The Moroccan Islamists: Challenge to the Monarchy)*, Paris, France: Découverte, 2005, pp. 283-285; "Mohamed Fizazi," Global Jihad website, available from *www.globaljihad.net/view_page.asp?id=390*; and McDermott, *Perfect Soldiers*, pp. 4-5, 87. A good indication of his views can be found in the following quotes from a year 2000 sermon at the al-Quds mosque:

> Who participates in the war against Islam with ideas or thoughts or a song or a television show to befoul Islam is an infidel on a war footing that shall be killed, no matter if it's a man, a woman, or a child. . . . The jihad for God's cause is hard for the infidels, because our religion has ordered us to cut their throats and that we kill their heirs. . .

Cited in *Ibid.*, p. 5. According to other sources, Zugham also personally visited the London residence of Muhammad al-Gharbuzi, the nominal head of the GICM, who he had become acquainted with through the Ibn Ya'ish brothers. See Alfonso Merlos, *Al Qaeda: Raíces y metas del terror global (Al Qaida: Roots and Aims of Global Terrorism)*, Madrid, Spain: Biblioteca Nueva, 2006, p. 210.

146. García-Abadillo, *11-M*, p. 122.

147. For Moroccan slums as a purported breeding ground for jihadism, see Andrea Elliot, "Where Boys Grow Up to Be Jihadis," *New York Times*, November 25, 2007, an article that nonetheless provides a good summary of Ahmidan's background and career. For the information in this paragraph, see further Marlasca and Rendueles, *Una historia del 11-M*, pp. 132-43; Webster and Orovio, *Conexión Madrid*, chaps. 3 and 5; and Irujo, *Agujero*, p. 269.

148. For more details about this incident, see Webster and Orovio, *Conexión Madrid*, pp. 57-58.

149. *Ibid.*, pp. 86-88, 93. It was also around this time that Bilal, his son with Rosa, was born.

150. *Ibid.*, pp. 88-90.

151. *Ibid.*, p. 89; Marlasca and Rendueles, *Una historia del 11-M*, p. 136.

152. Webster and Orovio, *Conexión Madrid*, p. 93; Elliot, "Where Boys Grow Up to Be Jihadis."

153. Webster and Orovio, *Conexión Madrid*, pp. 99-101.

154. *Ibid.*, pp. 101-2; Marlasca and Rendueles, *Una historia del 11-M*, pp. 137-139.

155. Webster and Orovio, *Conexión Madrid*, pp.133-134.

156. To mention only the most egregious example of his recklessness, on New Year's Eve of 2003-04 he drove up to Bilbao to confront another drug dealer who owed him money, located him at the Txikia bar in the Plaza de Zibalbaru, shot him in the knees with a pistol, then calmly exited and returned to Madrid. See Irujo, *Agujero*, p. 278.

157. See *Auto 10/04/06*, pp. 610-1125.

158. *Ibid.*, pp. 1241-1340.

159. Cf., e.g., the views expressed by Spanish political scientist Fernando Reinares, cited in "The 3/11 Madrid Bombings: An Assessment after 5 Years," Event Summary, Washington, DC:

Woodrow Wilson International Center for Scholars, April 6, 2009, available from *wilsoncenter.org/article/the-311-madrid-bombings-assessment-after-5-years.*

160. Irujo, *Agujero*, pp. 159-160, 243, and 274, note 1, citing a November 2, 2004, indictment issued by Judge Garzón against the Shuhada al-Maghribiyya (Martyrs of Morocco) group headed by Muhammad Ashraf. For more on the latter's plotting, see *Ibid.*, pp. 377-380.

161. For a judicious short summary of his activities, see Lia, *Architect of Global Jihad*, pp. 199-208.

162. Cf. Paul Cruickshank and Mohannad Hage Ali, "Abu Musab Al Suri: Architect of the New Al Qaeda," *Studies in Conflict and Terrorism*, Vol. 30, No. 1, January 2007, p. 9; and Lia, *Architect of Global Jihad*, pp. 200-201.

163. Cf. Maria Jesus Prades, "Spain Indicts Fugitive on 9/11 Charges," Associated Press, April 28, 2004; Irujo, *Agujero*, p. 159.

164. Lawrence Wright, "The Terror Web," *The New Yorker*, August 3, 2004, available from *www.newyorker.com/archive/2004/08/02/040802fa_fact.*

165. Cf. [Foreign Staff], "Madrid fugitive charged over 9/11," *The Scotsman*, April 28, 2004, available from *news.scotsman.com/internationalterrorism/Madrid-fugitive-charged-over-911.2524309.jp.* For more on Musawi and the projected "second wave" attacks, cf. Katherine C. Donahue, *Slave of Allah: Zacarias Moussaoui vs. the USA*, London, UK, and Ann Arbor, MI: Pluto, 2007; and Central Intelligence Agency, "Summary of Khalid Shaykh Muhammad Interrogation Testimony," pp. 37-40.

166. García-Abadillo, *11-M*, p. 112; Reinares, "3/11 Madrid Bombings"; *Declaración 07/11/06*, p. 14.

167. See *Declaración 07/11/06*, pp. 68-77.

168. *Sentencia 31/07/07*, pp. 639-643. Nevertheless, the sentence concluded, *Ibid.*, pp. 643-646, that although al-Hajj was identified on several relatives' and "brothers'" cell phones as "Abu Dujana," he was probably not the same person as Abu Dujan[a] al-Afghani,

who had claimed responsibility for the 3/11 attacks, since al-Hajj had never been a *mujahid* in Afghanistan. Hence he could not be convicted of being a planner of the Madrid bombings, *Ibid.*, pp. 646-647.

169. "La fecha del ataque del 11-M fue fijada al día siguiente de que Bin Laden amenazara a España" ("The Date of the 3/11 attack was fixed the day after Bin Ladin threatened Spain"), *El País*, August 5, 2005. It is well known that the jihadists like to select symbolic dates for their actions as well as use numerological systems, so much so that the Spanish CNI speculated, in a report entitled "Análisis de la teoría sobre el desarrollo histórico de los hechos que desembocan en el 11-M" ("Theoretical Analysis Concerning the Historical Development of the Facts that Led to 3/11"), that the 1921 year chosen could be associated with *sura* 21, *al-Anbiyya'* (The Prophets) of the *Qur'an*, whereas that of 1985 could be linked to *sura* 85, *al-Buruj* (The Stars). Note also the parallel case of Muhammad the Egyptian, who set up a Yahoo email account on February 4, 2004, using a phony name ("Muhammad Kishk") and a false date of birth (March 11, 1970) — 1 month before the 3/11 attacks! In this case also, Spanish analysts suspected that the incorrect year chosen for his birth date was an allusion to *sura* 70, *al-Ma'arij* (The Path of Ascension) of the *Qur'an*. See *Declaración 07/11/06*, p. 63 and note 2.

170. Apparently, this was the cover story used by visiting jihadists who were then involved in recruiting and funneling fighters into Iraq to resist the Americans. See Mohammed M. Hafez, *Suicide Bombers in Iraq: The Strategy and Ideology of Martyrdom*, Washington, DC: U.S. Institute of Peace, 2007, p. 198.

171. For the information in this paragraph, see *Declaración 07/11/06*, pp. 77-80. Cf. *Sentencia 31/07/07*, pp. 597-603, although the latter concluded (*Ibid.*, pp. 603-604) that despite his key position within the GICM, he had no role in the 3/11 attacks.

172. Some have also claimed that, at some point, Ahmad became affiliated with al-Takfir wa al-Hijra. See Irujo, *Agujero*, p. 198.

173. For the information in this paragraph, see Vidino, *Al Qaeda in Europe*, pp. 315-318, citing the 2004 Italian indictment

against Ahmad; and Irujo, *Agujero*, pp. 168-170. For a report on some of Ahmad's (secretly monitored) activities in Italy between April and June 2004, i.e., shortly after the Madrid bombings, see Questura di Milano, Divisione Investigazioni Generali ed Operazioni Speciali [DIGOS], Sezione Antiterrorismo, "Ricostruzione storica dell'attività di osservazione esterna sul conto di Rabei Osman El Sayed Ahmed, nato in Egitto il 22.07.1977, più altri a decorrere dal giorno 15 Aprile 2004" ("Historical Reconstruction of the External Surveillance Activities in relation to Rabei Osman El Sayed Ahmed, born in Egypt on 22 July 1977, starting from 15 April 2004"), June 3, 2004, pp. 1-7, prepared by Dario Martinelli.

174. *Ibid.*, p. 198.

175. Vidino, *Al Qaeda in Europe*, p. 310. The Italian police also determined that he was in Spain in December 2003. See *Declaración 07/11/06*, p. 62, note 100.

176. Irujo, *Agujero*, p. 244.

177. Vidino, *Al Qaeda in Europe*, pp. 311-312. For Italian translations and transcriptions of various phone calls made by Ahmad, see Questura di Milano, DIGOS, Sezione A, report in relation to Procedimento penale nr. 17596/04/Mod.21, "Esito attività investigativa nei confronti di Rabei Osman Ahmed El Sayed (alias Muhammad al-Masri) + 4," ("Historical Reconstruction of the External Surveillance Activities in relation to Rabei Osman El Sayed Ahmed, born in Egypt on 22 July 1977, starting from 15 April 2004"), June 5, 2004, pp. 16-42.

178. *Ibid.*, p. 313; *Auto 10/04/06*, pp. 64-65, note 104.

179. *Sentencia 31/07/07*, pp. 634-635. As is so often the case, however, the strained legal reasoning in this sentence with respect to Ahmad (*Ibid.*, pp. 630-636) interpreted the existing facts in such a way that the defendant was absolved of any serious crimes.

180. De Pablo, *Cuarta trama*, pp. 388-394. The 10 were Fakhit, al-'Azizi, al-Amari, Abu Mus'ab al-Suri, Abu Dahdah, Mu'taz and Muhannad al-Mallah, al-Haski, al-Hajj, and Muhammad the Egyptian.

181. Zeghal, *Islamistes marocains*, p. 275.

182. Merlos, *Al Qaeda*, p. 210.

183. *Ibid.*, p. 209.

184. *Ibid.*, pp. 217-218.

185. For a historical overview of the use of the term "leaderless resistance," see Chip Berlet, "The History, Definition, and Use of the Term 'Leaderless Resistance'," Public Eye website, undated available from *www.publiceye.org/liberty/terrorism/insurgency/leaderless-resistance.html*. See also Berlet's critiques of the application of this term by Hoffman and Sageman, "Leaderless Resistance and Right-Wing Insurgency: Sageman and Hoffman do not Accurately Describe the Role of Leaderless Resistance in Right-Wing Violence," Public Eye website, available from *www.publiceye.org/liberty/terrorism/insurgency/leaderless-resistance-right.html#sageman*. The closest parallels to "leaderless resistance"—and perhaps also "lone wolf" terrorism, a separate phenomenon—within the jihadist milieu are the ideas promoted by Abu Mus'ab al-Suri in his huge strategic treatise, *Da'wa al-muqawwama al-islamiyya al-'alamiyya (The Call for Global Islamic Resistance)*, Jihadi websites, December 2004, esp. pp. 1355-1413.

186. I make this claim on the basis of considerable first-hand experience, since during the past 20 years I have examined tens of thousands of pages of judicial materials dealing with terrorism cases, not only in several European countries but also in the United States. See, e.g., Jeffrey M. Bale, "The May 1973 Terrorist Attack at Milan Police Headquarters: Anarchist 'Propaganda of the Deed' or 'False Flag' Provocation?" *Terrorism and Political Violence*, Vol. 8, No. 1, Spring 1996, pp. 132-166.

187. To provide only a couple of illustrative examples, many guilty verdicts in Italy against neo-fascist terrorists and their secret service collaborators, verdicts often issued by left-wing judges, were subsequently overturned because these cases were later sent by political cronies within the judiciary to appellate courts in other jurisdictions with more conservative judges. The result was that, even in cases where there were vast amounts of reliable evidence against the accused, the defendants were often found innocent or, at best, convicted of lesser charges. For illustrative

examples, note the repeated trials of the neo-fascist defendants accused of carrying out the December 1969 Piazza Fontana bombing, who in the end were "absolved for lack of evidence." Forty years later, no one has yet been convicted of this crime.

188. A good example of this, which was also affected by the aforementioned problem, was the trial of numerous defendants in connection with the December 1970 "Borghese coup" in Rome. Although the initial sentence issued a guilty verdict and provided vast amounts of evidence indicating that many defendants were guilty of participating in an attempt to provoke a military coup, including the documented theft of six machine pistols from the armory of the Interior Ministry by neo-fascist participants from Avanguardia Nazionale (National Vanguard [AN]), in a second trial that decision was reversed on the basis of bizarre and wholly unconvincing legal reasoning.

189. For example, courts in various southern European countries that have the option of finding the defendants neither guilty nor innocent, but instead can absolve them for lack of evidence. In certain respects, this option is a good one for it enables the judges to cast doubt upon the defendants' innocence in cases where they do not really believe they are innocent but do not yet possess sufficient evidence to convict them, but at other times it allows judges to avoid making hard decisions by offering them an easy middle ground.

190. For example, the higher appellate courts in Britain, which appear to be staffed by civil libertarian zealots, have repeatedly overturned lower court verdicts against jihadist terrorist suspects. At this juncture, it is hard to even imagine what kinds of evidence they would consider sufficient to convict and severely punish Islamist terrorists. Apparently, they regard all of the defendants in these cases to be the innocent victims of "Islamophobia," irrespective of how much incriminating evidence exists.

191. It might, however, be of interest to compare and contrast features of the internal dynamics and intragroup interactions of jihadist groups, on the one hand, with those of other types of ideological extremist groups that do not place as much emphasis on kinship in recruiting, e.g., Marxist, anarchist, and neo-fascist groups.

192. The decision of the Spanish government to support the U.S. invasion of Iraq was only the latest in a long list of supposed "affronts" and international "aggressions" that led the cell members to view Spain as an enemy of Islam. After that decision, however, al-Shabli began talking about "killing the devil [José María] Aznar," who was then Prime Minister of Spain. See Marlasca and Rendueles, *Una historia del 11-M*, pp. 129-130.

193. As has been emphasized by De Arístegui, *Yihad en España*, chap. 4.

194. See, e.g., Williams, "In Cold Blood," pp. 22-24.

195. Marlasca and Rendueles, *Una historia del 11-M*, pp. 147-148.

196. *Sentencia 31/07/07*, p. 189.

197. *Ibid.*, pp. 189-190. Cf. García-Abadillo, *11-M*, pp. 116-118; Marlasca and Rendueles, *Una historia del 11-M*, pp. 159-169; De Pablo, *Cuarta trama*, p. 80.

198. Marlasca and Rendueles, *Una historia del 11-M*, pp. 155, 158-159.

199. For the information in this paragraph, cf. *Sentencia 31/07/07*, pp. 191-192; Marlasca and Rendueles, *Una historia del 11-M*, pp. 170-174; De Pablo, *Cuarta trama*, pp. 80-82.

200. For the information below, cf. *Sentencia 31/07/07*, pp. 192-196; Marlasca and Rendueles, *Una historia del 11-M*, pp. 174-176; García-Abadillo, *11-M*, pp. 119-120; De Pablo, *Cuarta trama*, pp. 82-85.

201. De Pablo, *Cuarta trama*, p. 87-88; Marlasca and Rendueles, *Una historia del 11-M*, pp. 176-178; García-Abadillo, *11-M*, p. 121.

202. *Sentencia 31/07/07*, pp. 197-199; Marlasca and Rendueles, *Una historia del 11-M*, pp. 178-182; García-Abadillo, *11-M*, pp. 122-123; De Pablo, *Cuarta trama*, pp. 88-91.

203. For the information in this paragraph, cf. *Sentencia 31/07/07*, pp. 199-200; Marlasca and Rendueles, *Una historia del 11-M*, pp. 182-183; De Pablo, *Cuarta trama*, pp. 91-98. Unfortunately, the latter author tries to explain this perplexing detour to Burgos by hypothesizing that Ahmidan and his crew went there to meet with persons who were involved in the "fourth plot" he claims existed, without providing any hard evidence. However, Ahmidan also stored some detonators in his Calle Villalobos flat, which was located in Madrid's Vallecas neighborhood. See García-Abadillo, *11-M*, p. 123.

204. *Sentencia 31/07/07*, p. 200.

205. Cf. Irujo, *Agujero*, pp. 267-269; Luis del Pino, *Los enigmas del 11-M: Conspiración o negligencia?* (*The Enigmas of 3/11: Conspiracy or Negligence?*), Madrid, Spain: Libros Libres, 2006, pp. 119-121. As the title indicates, Del Pino is yet another author promoting a conspiratorial perspective on the Madrid bombings. Even so, his description of the ownership and succession of renters of the Chinchón property is among the clearest and most concise.

206. García-Abadillo, *11-M*, p. 122.

207. De Pablo, *Cuarta trama*, pp. 112-114.

208. Cf. *Auto 10/04/06*, pp. 205, 207; Marlasca and Rendueles, *Una historia del 11-M*, pp. 99, 146-147; Ernesto Milà, *11-M, los perros del infierno: En el terrorismo internacional nada es que parece* (*3/11, The Dogs of Hell [or The Hellhounds]: Nothing is What it Appears to be in International Terrorism*), Barcelona, Spain: Pyre, 2004, pp. 84, 107, chart). Note that the latter author is a veteran neo-fascist radical whose conspiratorial book disputes the official version and argues that the Madrid bombings were the product of a state-sponsored "false flag" terrorist attack. Hence although he provides some useful bits of information, his main objective is to challenge various factual claims presented by the government or published in the "establishment" media.

209. Irujo, *Agujero*, p. 367.

210. Marlasca and Rendueles, *Una historia del 11-M*, pp. 145, 181, including note 73). The title of this manual was "Chain of Preparations for the Struggle."

211. Cf. Emerson Vermaat, "Madrid Terrorism Trial Verdict," electronic p. 4; and Irujo, *Agujero*, p. 244, where it is claimed that Muhammad provided secret information on bomb making to Fakhit and his group (after which they practiced in the Chinchón house) and p. 368; and Agence France-Presse, "Saad Husseini, posible artificiero de las bombas del 11-M, condenado a 15 años por los atentados de Casablanca de 2003" ("Saad Husseini, possible fabricator of the 3/11 bombs, condemned to 15 years in prison for the 2003 Casablanca attacks"), *El País*, February 27, 2009, available from *3diasdemarzo.blogspot.com/2009/02/saad-husseini-posible-artificie o-de.html*. Note that the latter was also the presumed bomb maker in the Casablanca attacks as well. Judge Juan Del Olmo suspected him of being the "inventor" of the backpack bombs used on 3/11.

212. De Pablo, *Cuarta trama*, pp. 111-120, 397-399. Unfortunately, as I have noted elsewhere, there is a large and ever-growing conspiratorial literature on the 3/11 bombings, a literature which ranges from the utterly delusional to the suggestive but inconclusive. For an example of the former, see Bruno Cardeñosa, *11-M: Claves de una conspiración* (*Keys to a Conspiracy*), Madrid, Spain: Espejo de Tinta, 2004.

213. For the information in the above paragraph, see Andreas Ulrich, "Ticket to Iraq," *Der Spiegel*, April 7, 2007. I was unable to retrieve the original German version from the magazine's website.

214. Hubert Gude, "'Von Gott belohnt'" ("Rewarded by God"), *Focus Magazin*, January 8, 2007, available from *www.focus.de/politik/deutschland/terror-von-gott-belohnt_aid_224850.html*.

215. For the absurd overreactions to the publications of cartoons satirizing Muhammad, overreactions that were not spontaneous but rather were systematically fomented, fueled, and organized by Islamist agitators, see Mohamed Sifaoui, *L'affaire des caricatures: Dessins et manipulations* (*The Cartoons Affair: Designs and Manipulations*), Privé, 2006, esp. chaps. 4-5. The key figure in generating the worldwide Muslim hysteria about these cartoons was a radical cleric residing in Denmark named Ahmad Abu Laban, who even went so far as to sponsor the production of phony Muhammad cartoons in order to inflame Muslim passions. Per-

haps the most shameful aspect of this entire affair, however, was the unwillingness of most Western newspapers, including in the United States, to reprint those cartoons in the interests of resisting Islamist intimidation and defending free speech.

216. Ulrich, "Ticket to Iraq."

217. What is clear is that al-Hajj Dib downloaded the afore-mentioned video from a website—a video 12 minutes long which had an Arabic-language narration—and simply tried to follow the instructions provided therein. However, chemists at the Bundeskriminalamt (BKA) believed that the video, which purported to depict the various steps one had to follow to make homemade bombs, lacked certain vitally important information that limited its usefulness for novices unfamiliar with pressurized gases.

218. *Ibid.*

219. *Ibid.* However, these tests were later criticized for being overly academic and unrealistic, since the German experts used various techniques and equipment that were not available to the would-be bombers. See Gerd Elendt, "Staatsfeind Nummer Eins" ("Public Enemy Number One"), *Der Stern*, December 13, 2007, pp. 74ff.

220. Herbert Gude and Josef Hufelschulte, "Eine Art Napalm" ("A Type of Napalm"), *Focus Magazin* [Munich], September 12, 2006, pp. 42-43.

221. Elendt, "Staatsfeind Nummer Eins."

222. "Die Bomben waren dilettantisch gebaut" ("The bombs were amateurishly constructed"), *Der Spiegel* online, August 21, 2006, available from *www.spiegel.de/panorama/justiz/0,1518,432782,00.html.* In contrast, however, a BKA bomb disposal expert claimed that the bombs were constructed very professionally. See "Zeuge: Kofferbomber hätten ein Inferno aus-gelöst" ("Witness: Suitcase bombers had planned an inferno"), *Die Welt*, February 20, 2007.

223. Gude, "'Von Gott belohnt'."

224. For the general history and characteristics of Hizb al-Tahrir, see especially Suha Taji-Farouki, *A Fundamental Quest: Hizb al-Tahrir and the Search for the Islamic Caliphate,* London, UK: Grey Seal, 1996, an outstanding monographic study. Compare also Zeyno Baran, ed., *The Challenge of Hizb ut-Tahrir: Deciphering and Radical Islamist Ideology. Conference Report,* Washington, DC: Nixon Center, 2004; and Emmanuel Karagiannis and Clark McCauley, "Hizb-ut-Tahrir al-Islami: Evaluating the Threat Posed by a Radical Islamic Group that Remains Nonviolent," *Terrorism and Political Violence,* Vol. 18, No. 2, July 2006, pp. 315-334. For further evidence of Hizb's ideological radicalism, compare also its numerous publications, many of which are available in PDF format on the group's own website, available from *www.hizbuttahrir.org.*

225. Peter Finn, "Germany Bans Islamic Group," *Washington Post,* January 16, 2003. HT has since challenged that ban, both in Germany (to no avail) and in the European court. Cf. Richard Bernstein, "Islamic group challenges ban on its organizing activities in Germany," *International Herald Tribune,* September 27, 2004; and Ian Cobain, "Islamist group challenges Berlin's five-year ban in European court," *The Guardian* [London], June 24, 2008, available from *www.guardian.co.uk/world/2008/jun/24/islam.religion.*

226. Knut Krohn, "Einzeltäter oder Teil eines Terrornetzwerkes? Ein Kofferbomber soll Verbindungen zu Islamisten haben" ("Lone actor or part of a terrorist network? Suitcase bomber must have links to Islamists"), *Stuttgarter Zeitung,* August 24, 2006.

227. See Gude, "'Von Gott belohnt'"; Florian Harms and Alexander Schwabe, "Kiels Nährboden für Islamisten" ("Kiel's breeding ground for Islamists"), *Der Spiegel,* August 25, 2006; and Philip Eppelsheim, "Norddeutsche Al Qaida Connection?" ("North German Al Qaida Connection?"), *Frankfurter Allgemeine Zeitung,* July 24, 2007. Yet even that particular mosque was apparently not radical enough for Ridwan, since he had a dispute with its imam 'Abd al-Majid al-Samadawi over the 7/7 bombings, which the former publicly supported. See *Ibid.* Note also that Sa'id bin al-Hajji has also been linked to members of the 3/11 cell.

228. Andreas Ulrich, "Failed Bomb Plot Seen as Al-Qaida Initiation Test," *Der Spiegel*, September 4, 2007, available from *www.spiegel.de/international/germany/0,1518,476238,00.html*.

229. For the background and context of the development of Sunni jihadist groups in Lebanon, see Bernard Rougier, *Everyday Jihad: The Rise of Militant Islam among Palestinians in Lebanon*, Cambridge, MA, and London, UK: Harvard University, 2009, esp. chap. 7.

230. "Suspect in Lebanon Bomb Plot Killed in Lebanon Fighting," Deutsche Welle, May 21, 2007, available from *www.dw-world.de/dw/article/0,2144,2546292,00.html*; "Failed German Train Suspect Killed in Lebanon," Associated Press, May 21, 2007, available from *www.foxnews.com/printer_friendly_story/0,3566,274154,00.html*.

231. Peter R. Neumann, "Europe's Jihadist Dilemma," *Survival*, Vol. 48, No. 2, Summer 2006, p. 77.

232. This does not mean, of course, that al-Qa'ida Central was involved.

233. For more on this case, cf. J. A. Emerson Vermaat, *De Hofstadgroep: Portrat van een radical-islamitisch netwerk* (*The Hofstad Group: Portrait of a Radical Islamist Network*), Soesterberg, The Netherlands: Aspekt, 2005; *Nederlandse Jihad: Het proces tegen de Hofstadgroep* (*Jihad in the Netherlands: The Trial against the Hofstad Group*), Soesterberg, The Netherlands: Aspekt, 2007; Lorenzo Vidino,"The Hofstad Group: The New Face of Terrorist Networks in Europe," *Studies in Conflict and Terrorism*, Vol. 30, No. 7, 2007, pp. 579-592. Members of the Hofstadgroep had documented links to other jihadist cells in Europe, and some may have also forged links to terrorist organizations in Pakistan. Hence characterizing them as "unconnected" would be problematic.

www.ingramcontent.com/pod-product-compliance
Lightning Source LLC
Chambersburg PA
CBHW070652290526
45790CB00001B/284